Learning to Sail

Learning to Sail

with Bob Fisher

237

CAXTON EDITIONS

Dedication
For Edward and Catherine Archer, and
Christopher Matthews

This Edition Published 2000 by
Caxton Editions an Imprint of
The Caxton Publishing Group

Copyright © 1996
Regency House Publishing Limited

Text copyright © 1996 Bob Fisher
The right of Bob Fisher to be identified as the
author of his work has been asserted by him
in accordance with the Copyright, Design and
Patents Act, 1988.

ISBN 1 84067 119X

Printed in Italy

Acknowledgements
All illustrations are supplied by
Edmunds and Hunt Advertising with the
exception of the line drawings on pages 13,
51 which are by Publishing Workshop.

Buoy and chart diagrams on pages 72, 73,
75, 75, 76 are published courtesy of the
Hydrographic office as published in the
International Association off Lighthouse
Authorities' *Maritime Buoyage System*.

*Pages 2-3: Hooked on Speed,
Keith Musto's Melges 24 at the
British National Championship.*

*These pages: Cowes Week
attracts all types of yachts.*

CONTENTS

PREFACE

All too frequently, while attracted to the idea of learning to sail, people are put off by the jargon. Why, they ask, are there so many terms, all seemingly different, for what appear to be very similar items on a boat? Why do we call the right-hand side of a boat starboard and the left-hand port? This is not some kind of arcane language devised to confuse, but terms which have evolved through usage and which continue to be used to prevent confusion.

The terms port and starboard will almost certainly disappear, as they already have in the U.S. Navy, because they no longer have need of this kind of terminology to describe the parts of the boat. It does seem strange, how-

ever, to hear talk of the left tack and the right tack, and this fact alone provides a slight hope that use of the original terms may still persist. Most other nautical terms, however, exist to describe accurately and precisely the parts of the boat and her rig.

Throughout this book, the proper terms are used and are described in the glossary; boats are referred to as 'she' and sailors 'he'. This is not a sign of chauvinism on my part for I consider myself to have done rather more than most of my contemporaries to encourage women to sail and race competitively. It is merely a means to greater economy and clarity.

Sailing is a sport to be enjoyed, and it can be by anyone from three to ninety-three. From a basic learned knowledge, experience gained afloat will soon turn a beginner into a worthwhile sailor ready to tackle the challenge of the sport.

INTRODUCTION

Roddy Bridge and Adrian Murphy in perfect balance with their International 14 – pure concentrated fun.

To be able to sail at all, let alone properly, one must have some comprehension of what is involved in driving a boat through the water. It isn't simply a matter of wind blowing on the sails and the boat being pushed along in front of it; that early concept has long been superseded. At first, the theory of sailing may seem a complex physical equation, but on closer examination it encompasses a few simple facts which can be readily assimilated.

It must be understood that the wind travels horizontally across a sail, which, in turn, adopts an aerofoil shape similar to the wing of an aircraft. Had the early sailors been familiar with the theory of flight, they would have invented more sophisticated rigs for the windjammers, and had the early aviators appreciated what really happened on sailing boats, they might have been airborne earlier. The flow of the wind across the sail is deflected by the sail creating a difference in pressure be-tween the two sides, which, in turn, provide a force whose vectors describe forward motion in the boat.

This force is further complicated by the action of the water on the keel or centreboard and the hull of the boat. Further forces are created which prevent the boat from slipping sideways and provide an additional forward impetus, helping the boat to slide through the water.

Knowing exactly what happens when the wind hits the sails will help the novice to appreciate why he must do certain things and why, in the cause of efficiency, he must do them in a prescribed order. Sailing is nothing if not logical and it follows that an illogical approach will prove next to useless. Getting it wrong could result in nothing more serious than stopping the boat, but there could equally be more dangerous repercussions. The elemental forces of wind and waves can be relentlessly powerful and this is a compelling reason why care on board must be exercised at all times.

The ability to swim has long been considered essential for all

going to sea in boats, but it is not a prerequisite as long as a personal buoyancy aid is worn at all times. If being a non-swimmer were a bar to sailing, it is unlikely that the world's most famous sailor, Dennis Conner, would ever have gone afloat. To this day, the four-time winner of the America's Cup is still a non-swimmer.

Sailing is a sport for both sexes of all ages and there is a place for people of every level of talent and physical ability. There is nothing to prevent the physically handicapped from taking part and, indeed, many are discovering sailing as the ideal sport, both for recreation and competition. In addition, the blind are increasingly mastering the necessary techniques to enable them to partake in sailing activities.

General awareness of the part the weather can play, both in its major as well as minor changes of mood is sailing's equivalent of 'keeping one's eye on the ball'. Beecher Moore, who sailed for many years with the designer and boatbuilder, Jack Holt, said of his partner, 'Jack always knows what the wind is going to do. In his feeling for the wind, as well as wood and water, he's very close to nature.' Jack and Beecher were a highly successful team, providing opportunities for hundreds of thousands to sail small boats and, having had multiple racing successes of their own, were their own best advertisement.

Being aware of both weather and tidal changes is as important to the potterer as it is to the Olympic sailor. Choosing an incorrect course of action can be dangerous and failing to under-

stand significant changes in the elements could even prove fatal. A close affinity with nature and the ability to detect minute fluctuations in sky, sea and wind should be developed as much as possible. As Arthur Ransome's Captain John observed as he sailed *Swallow* (in *Swallows and Amazons*), 'You are watching the dark patches on the water that show you a harder puff is coming and you have to be ready at any moment to slacken the sheet or to luff up into the wind.'

Anyone can learn to sail and there are aspects of sailing to interest everyone. Age is no barrier in either direction and whether you are seven, seventeen or seventy there is still time to start from scratch. The most important thing for the beginner to remember is to set themselves achievable goals.

You will need the perseverance to apply yourself to these a step at a time and do not be disappointed if your progress is not as rapid as you would like.

One may have daydreams of winning an Olympic gold medal or of skippering an America's Cup challenger – much in the same way as every golfer dreams of shooting a round five under par – but there is no earthly reason why a beginner in May cannot win a club race 12 months hence, or be skippering his own boat in a cross-Channel cruise the following summer.

There are definite steps along the way and many ways of taking them, whether they be under the aegis of a professional sailing school, as part of a club programme, or simply in the hands of an accomplished friend. Fifty

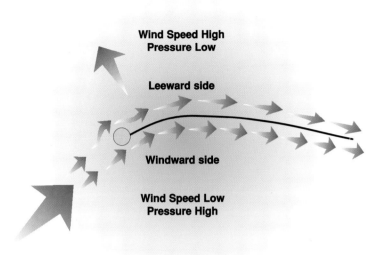

Wind Speed High
Pressure Low

Leeward side

Windward side

Wind Speed Low
Pressure High

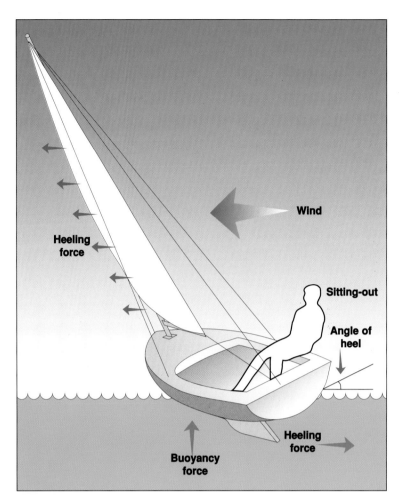

Wind

Heeling
force

Sitting-out

Angle of
heel

Heeling
force

Buoyancy
force

ABOVE
What gives a sailing boat propulsion – the pressure difference caused by the air flowing over the curved sail with the wind on the leeward side able to travel faster than the air on the windward side.

LEFT
Shirley Robertson sailing her Europe Class dinghy off Miami, just five months before she was due to represent Britain in the Olympic Games for the second time. To reach Shirley's standard needs considerable dedication, but there are other standards in the sport for those who wish less involvement.

TOP RIGHT
The forces involved with a sailing boat – the wind on the sails causes it to heel as does the pressure on the keel or centreboard while the buoyancy of the hull helps to balance these together with the sitting out force of the crew.

BELOW RIGHT
The component forces of the sails.
(A) is the leeway force component, which is counteracted by the resistance of the keel or centreboard (B)
(C) is the forward component of the lift from the sail (D).

years ago, it was very different; the only way to learn then was by one's own mistakes, and while there is some value in this, especially in the early days, there are now genuine sources of information designed to help the sailor improve his skills.

One word of warning is necessary, however; the experience of sailing should be tried for the first time on a fine day when it is warm and pleasant and there is a decent breeze, preferably in the company of a competent companion. Any deviation from this policy can bring swift, unnecessary disillusionment or even fear guaranteed to mar the experience forever. Getting wet, cold and uncomfort-

able may be inevitable later on, but unless the first impression of sailing is favourable and the rudiments explained in a clear and encouraging way, an overwhelming desire to quit before it is too late may well be generated.

Go to it, therefore, cheerily. Sailing is there to be enjoyed and is a sport or recreation to last all one's life. There is something for everyone, even for the person whose main object is to possess a boat in pristine condition; one who likes nothing better than to spend eleven-and-a-half months a year working on her and the other two weeks worrying when he is afloat and under way. Above all, sailing should be fun.

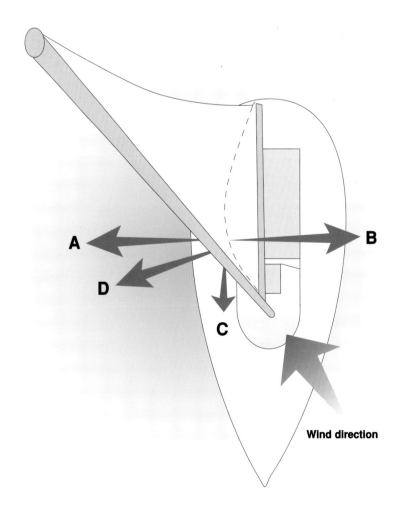

A

B

D

C

Wind direction

CHAPTER ONE
Sailing Terminology
What's in a Name?

One of the complaints beginners make about sailing is that there are so many terms to learn and that it appears to have an unnecessary jargon all its own. This jargon does not exist simply to bewilder the unwary but to ensure that when orders are issued no confusion or misunderstanding can possibly arise. Each individual part of a boat is specifically named so that communication can be immediately understood, and there is a directional terminology as well. At first, these may baffle the novice but, once learned, they will provide the basis for easy comprehension and immediate and correct response.

The basic structure of a boat is simple. The bow is at the front and the stern is at the back. The part of the hull which is underwater is the underbody and the topsides are that part of the hull which is above water, the largely horizontal 'top' being the deck. It is steered by means of a tiller (sometimes a wheel) which is attached to the rudder. Most usually, there is an extension to the tiller, connected by means of a universal joint, known as the tiller extension, which enables the helmsman to sit on the side of the boat to steer. To provide stability and resistance to slipping sideways, there is either a keel or a daggerboard/centreboard.

The driving force is the rig, complemented by the underwater shape of the hull and the foils (keel or daggerboard/centreboard). The mast is supported by the standing rigging – generally of wire, sometimes made of steel rod – and the sails are controlled by the running rigging – generally ropes, but never called that. Ropes are, in general, called lines, but each individual one will have its own specific name. These are called sheets, guys, halyards and lifts, among others.

Most of the terms, if examined, are nothing more than descriptive and should certainly not be a source of confusion. It is necessary to master them, but the beginner should not expect to learn them all at once. They will, however, find their way about a boat much more easily once a reasonable grasp of the terminology has been obtained. This does not mean one should rush to learn the name of each small fitting on deck, but a good knowledge of the general terms should be acquired in order to fully understand instructions.

Directions are of singular importance. Forward (fore) and aft (at or near the stern) are reasonably easy to understand, as is below (never downstairs), which

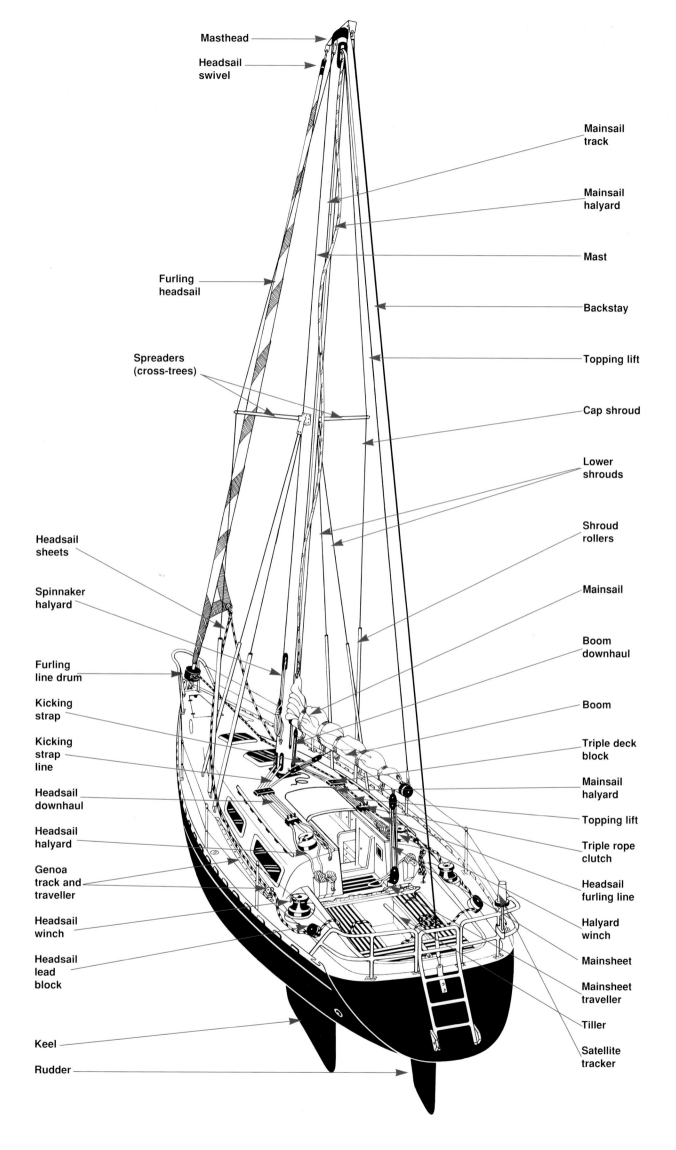

Masthead

Headsail
swivel

Furling
headsail

Spreaders
(cross-trees)

Headsail
sheets

Spinnaker
halyard

Furling
line drum

Kicking
strap

Kicking
strap
line

Headsail
downhaul

Headsail
halyard

Genoa
track and
traveller

Headsail
winch

Headsail
lead
block

Keel

Rudder

Mainsail
track

Mainsail
halyard

Mast

Backstay

Topping lift

Cap shroud

Lower
shrouds

Shroud
rollers

Mainsail

Boom
downhaul

Boom

Triple deck
block

Mainsail
halyard

Topping lift

Triple rope
clutch

Headsail
furling line

Halyard
winch

Mainsheet

Mainsheet
traveller

Tiller

Satellite
tracker

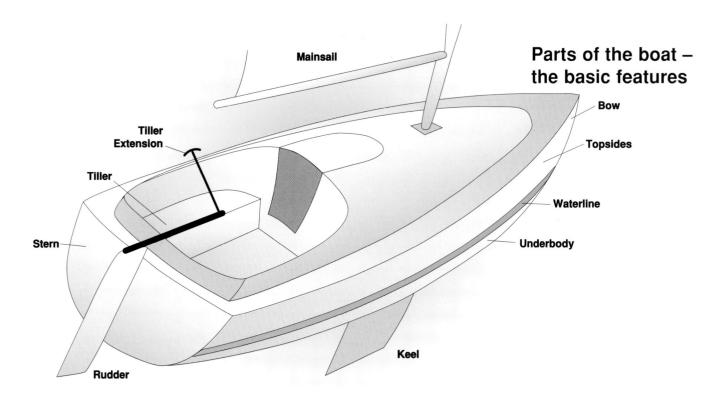

Parts of the boat – the basic features

Mainsail

Bow

Topsides

Tiller Extension

Tiller

Waterline

Underbody

Stern

Keel

Rudder

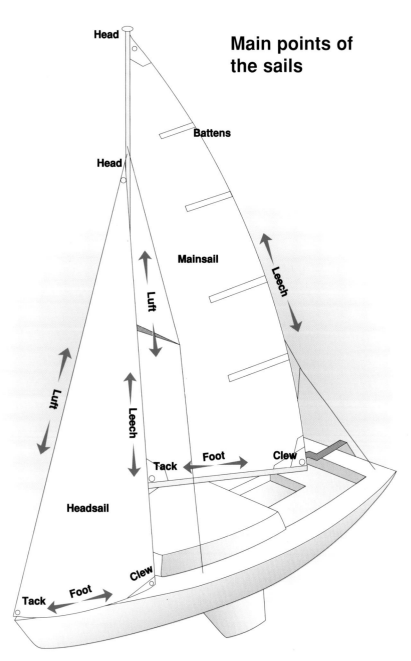

Main points of the sails

Head

Battens

Head

Mainsail

Leech

Luft

Luft

Leech

Foot

Clew

Tack

Headsail

Clew

Tack

Foot

Luft

means under the deck or in the cabin. Other positions of a boat are described as ahead (obvious), astern (behind), on the port or starboard (left or right) quarter (in the quadrant aft of abeam, [at right angles to the boat's widest point]), or on the port or starboard bow (in the quadrant ahead of abeam). A boat has a windward and leeward (pronounced loo'ard) side – the former being the side towards the wind and the latter the side which faces away. Windward and leeward are clearly defined either side of the centreline of the boat and are not necessarily at right angles to the wind (they rarely are). Most generally, because a boat heels to the force of the wind, the windward side is higher than the leeward one.

Many of the less obvious terms in sailing derive from the person who first used them or from their place of origin. A big headsail – the triangular sail forward of the mast – is known as a genoa, because the sail first saw the light of day at a regatta off the Italian port of Genoa. The cringle in the luff of a mainsail, just above the boom into which a downward tackle is inserted, is known as the

Cunningham hole, after its inventor, Briggs Cunningham.

Sails are, on the whole, easy to name. The mainsail, generally the biggest used when going to windward, is set aft of the main mast. Headsails – genoas, jibs and staysails – are all triangular and set forward of the mast. Genoas and jibs (which are smaller and do not overlap the mast like genoas) are set on the forestay, the piece of standing rigging which goes from the stem of the boat to the top, or near the top, of the mast. Staysails are set behind jibs.

If the boat has two masts and the aft mast is smaller, it is known as the mizzen mast and the sails set from it are the mizzen (aft of the mast) and mizzen staysails (forward of the mast).

Large, lightweight sails used when going downwind are called spinnakers (the origin of this name is highly disputed) and can be set from the main and mizzen masts. It was the enormous extra power of the mizzen spinnakers on the 80-foot ketches in the Whitbread Round the World Race that returned the two-masted rig to a brief popularity.

Each sail has its various parts.

Points of direction

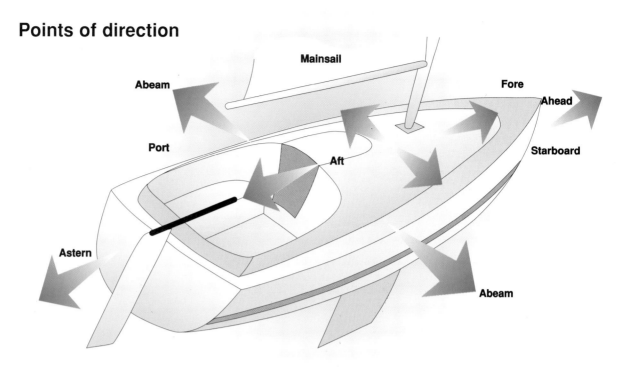

The Beneteau 42s7, Skandia
Life, a modern cruiser/racer
whose crew is enjoying regatta
sailing. Look closely just back
from the luff of the jib to note the
tell-tales streaming aft on both
sides of the sail, indicating that it
is properly set for the direction
of the wind.

The forward edge is the luff, the aft edge is the leech and the bottom edge is the foot. Symmetrical spinnakers have two leeches and a foot, while the sides of asymmetric spinnakers are as for other sails. The three corners of a sail also have names; the one at the top is the head, at the bottom of the forward edge is the tack and at the other end of the foot, at the bottom of the leech, is the clew.

Because few sails have straight leeches, they are fitted with battens made from wood or plastics, to support the extra curve, which is known as the roach. The battens are slipped into pockets on the outside of the sail.

Almost without exception, the foot of the mainsail will be attached to the boom, a spar made of wood, aluminium alloy tube or fibre reinforced plastics, similar in construction to the mast. It joins the mast with a universal joint – the gooseneck. The boom has an adjustable tackle rigged about 25 per cent of its length from the mast to the foot of the mast to stop it skying (rising when it swings outwards). This is known as the vang or kicking strap.

The mast is supported by one or more forestays, the principle one being the most forward and the others, if present, being known, naturally, as inner forestays. Sideways, the mast is supported by shrouds, which may be spread by cross-trees or spreaders. There may be more than one shroud on each side of the mast and some racing yachts have linked rigging over as many as five spreaders on each side of the mast. In addition, there may be one or more backstays. The standing backstay (of wire or rod) goes from the top of the mast to the stern of the boat, while the running backstays (of wire or high modulus synthetic fibre), one on either side, if present, are

attached to the mast at the same height as the forestay. There may also be checkstays, one or more per side, attached at various points lower down the mast.

The sails are hoisted by halyards, made of wire or rope, or wire and rope. The use of non-stretch synthetic fibre rope is becoming universal for halyards in all types of boats from dinghies to large ocean racers.

There are five main points of sailing. A boat is said to be close-hauled when it is sailing as close towards the wind as possible (somewhere near 45 degrees to the direction of the wind). When the boat is pointed slightly further away from the wind, it is close-

reaching. When the wind is almost at right angles to the direction of the boat, it is beam-reaching; further off still and it is broad-reaching. With the wind almost dead astern, a boat is said to be running.

When the boat is close-hauled, the sails are trimmed nearest the centreline and the further the boat is pointed away from the wind the more the sheets (the lines which control the sails), are eased so that when running the boom is almost square to the fore and aft line of the boat.

When the wind is coming from the right-hand side of the boat, it is said to be on starboard tack; if from the left-hand side, it is on

port tack. This is true no matter how far the boat is off the wind. Turning from port tack to starboard tack, bringing the wind right on the bow in the process, is known as tacking. Changing from one tack to another with the wind aft – providing a possibly dangerous scenario in strong winds – is known as gybing.

ABOVE
The Victory class, Janet, *reaching under spinnaker at Cowes Week.*

RIGHT
The Whitbread Race winner, Steinlager 2, *does the same, but twice – one on each mast – at the start of the final leg from Fort Lauderdale to Southampton.*

CHAPTER TWO
Getting the Feel

In the Beginning...

The first steps, taken somewhat gingerly, in learning to sail should be taken with someone who knows and understands the theory and can impart this knowledge without making it seem like a mass of instructions, lists of names and a welter of warnings. Go afloat with such a person in a relatively stable boat (not so stable that you gain nothing from the experience) and see exactly how they handle her. In no time at all, the instructor will be offering you, the beginner, an opportunity to steer.

He will have set the boat up on a beam reach, with the wind at 90 degrees to the course on what is known as a 'soldier's wind' because sailors believe that under these conditions, even a soldier can steer a straight course! The novice will soon discover that 'even a soldier' needs a degree of competency to avoid a wiggly wake – what sailors refer to as the helmsman writing his name behind the boat. It will, after a few minutes, prove not too difficult to keep the boat pointing in the right direction.

The beginner should look for some point, on the shore or a buoy, to steer for so that he can see what happens to the boat when he moves the tiller. Pushing the tiller to the right makes the rudder angle to the left and the boat will turn to the left; pushing it to the left makes the boat turn to the right. Movement of the tiller should be gentle but firm, never abrupt or jerky. The instructor should tack the boat and the novice steer her on a reciprocal course (back to the starting point) on the other tack. When the boat begins to run out of sea room, the novice should attempt to tack the boat and set her on a beam reach on the other tack, the instructor giving advice on how to do this. A boat with a wheel, although not recommended, is easier for the complete novice to handle as the head of the boat will follow the turn of the wheel like a motor-car.

After an hour of this, by which time the beginner should no longer be one but should have achieved some idea of the basic skills necessary to steer a sailing boat, they should go ashore and examine the whole procedure. Discussion, preferably with diagrams, will give the pupil the opportunity to seek answers to the many questions that will immediately spring to mind.

Stage two is more of the same. There just isn't any substitute for time at the tiller for gaining confidence and the 'feel' of a boat. Getting the feel is of paramount

The Sigma 400, Independent Bear, with a light genoa set. Note the crew to leeward to encourage the boat to heel in the light wind in order to give some 'feel' on the helm.

DIAGRAM
With the sails trimmed to sail the 'proper course', the tell-tales on the jib show deviation from that course, or a wind change. On course, the tell-tales on both sides should stream aft; sail too high and the windward one collapses; sail too low and the leeward one will flutter.

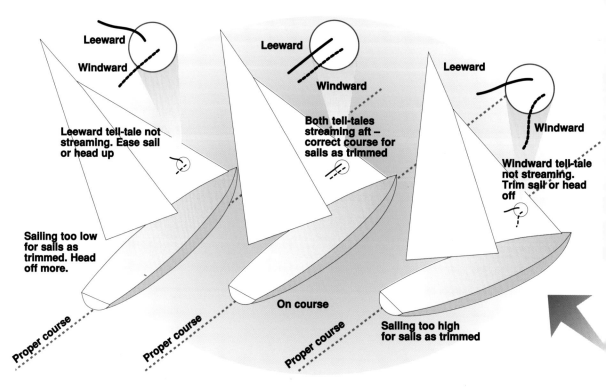

Leeward
Windward
Leeward tell-tale not streaming. Ease sail or head up
Sailing too low for sails as trimmed. Head off more.
Proper course

Leeward
Windward
Both tell-tales streaming aft – correct course for sails as trimmed
On course
Proper course

Leeward
Windward
Windward tell-tale not streaming. Trim sail or head off
Sailing too high for sails as trimmed
Proper course

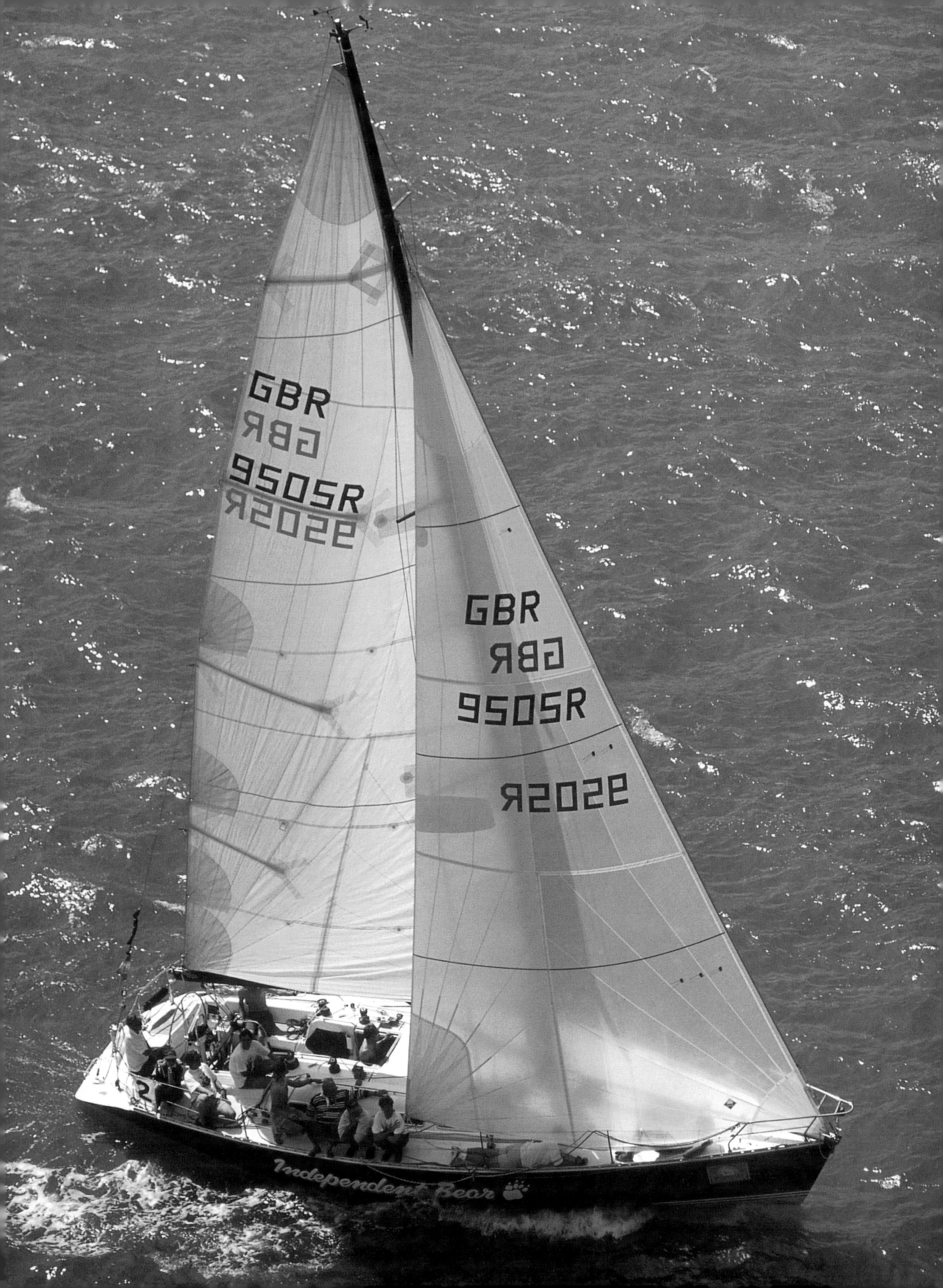
GBR
9505R
GBR
9505R
Independent Bear

importance to securing mastery of the technique of sailing. The same is true of a car, a bicycle, and even a horse; it is the co-ordination of hand and eye that comes with experience, the transmission of the sensation of sailing to the body and mind of the sailor. Without that 'feel' the sailor can never be fully aware of what it really means to sail a boat.

On the initial sailing trip, the instructor will trim the sails himself; there is simply too much for the beginner to comprehend at this early stage; but once he is afloat for the second time and has begun to sail steadily, the time is ripe to commence the second stage of instruction, that of setting the sails to the wind. Because each sail is an aerofoil, they must be trimmed so that neither sail is stalling, but it must be understood that in the normal two-sail configuration, each one is related to the other and the flow of air over the rig is correspondingly complex. For this reason, many instructors find it best to set only the mainsail in the early stages of teaching a person to sail.

We will follow this method and thus simplify an early appreciation of wind flow. Setting up on a beam reach, with the wind at 90 degrees to the course, there will be signs of where the wind is coming from which the sailor must understand. The flag or indicator at the top of the mast will show, once the boat is under way, that the apparent wind, the wind that flows over the rig, is coming from ahead of the true wind, the wind blowing over the water, because the boat is moving forwards. The experienced sailor is always aware of the apparent wind direction and will not even need to look to the masthead – he will feel it on his face.

As the boat sails along on its course, the beginner should be encouraged to ease and trim the mainsheet and watch what effect it has. Easing it out too far will result in the forward third of the sail beginning to collapse and the cloth inverting. The sail is now stalled and the aerofoil shape lost. It is now unable to produce the maximum effect needed to drive the boat forward. If it is pulled in too far, there will be a greater heeling effect which can be clearly seen if the sail has tell-tales of wool – visual aids attached to its surface. On the leeward side, the threads of wool will flicker to face forward. They will do this on the windward side when the sail is over-eased. The idea is to keep the tell-tales on each side streaming aft.

After a while, the beginner should have mastered the technique of sailing in a straight line on a beam reach while trimming the sail to minor shifts in the wind: he will soon realize that only rarely does the breeze remain totally stable for any appreciable time and that to obtain maximum efficiency from the sail – with tell-tales on both sides streaming nicely – the sheet needs to be constantly trimmed.

It is at this point that the beginner must subject himself to a little self-examination. He needs to ask himself if he is the sort of person to enjoy sailing wholeheartedly. Will he be able to master the necessary skills involved? Unless the answers to both these questions are 'yes', there is very little point in progressing further. Before making a final decision he may wish to repeat the experience once more, remembering that there are very few who, having committed themselves thus far, will not aim to succeed. There are some, however, who are just not cut out for a life afloat and they would be better advised to find some other pastime to enjoy.

Teasing the most out of an Enterprise sailing downwind in light airs, the crew holds the clew of the jib in an effort to help it set.

CHAPTER THREE
The Theory of Sailing
Onwards and Upwards

Sailing at its very best – two Solings approaching the windward mark at the pre-Olympic Regatta at Savannah.

Sailing to windward is unnatural. It is easy to comprehend why boats go with the wind, but why they should sail to any degree into it needs explanation. First, the sails are not simply there to block the wind, take its pressure, and convert it into a force in line with that wind. They are foils, like the wings of a glider, and the air flows across them, faster on the leeward side, creating a pressure difference – lower on the leeward side than it is on the windward side.

This pressure difference creates a lift force, just like that of an aeroplane's wing, which is pushed through the air by the force generated by its engines. In the case of a boat sail, the wind alone provides the air flow, but as the boat starts to move because of the pressure generated, that airflow is altered and its angle to the boat is changed. The flow across the sail is known as the apparent wind – the true wind's velocity – to which is added the further vector of the boat's movement.

The apparent wind speed may be increased or diminished, depending on the angle of the true wind to the boat. If the apparent wind is from ahead of the beam, it will show as an increased speed on the boat's instruments, should it be so equipped. Light and highly responsive boats may

start with a true wind blowing from well aft of the beam, pick up speed and bring it well forward. Catamarans, for example, have their sails well sheeted in for most of the time, and ice-yachts, which achieve remarkably high speeds, have their sails quickly sheeted home once they are under way as they are almost always sailing with the apparent wind close hauled. You can see this by watching the flag or indicator at the mast head as the sails are sheeted on and the boat begins to move from stationary.

Underwater, the centreboard or keel and the rudder act similarly to provide a lift component. The force of the wind causes the boat to heel while the weight of keel and crew serve as a counterbalance thus righting the boat. These latter, together with the buoyancy of the hull, force the sails against the wind. Together, they provide a squeezing force on the hull which helps to propel the sailing craft through the water. Add the driving force of the sails and the boat will sail as close as 45 degrees to the direction from which the true wind is blowing. Some racing yachts, because of their efficient hull shapes and their rigs, will achieve as much as 10 degrees closer than this, but 45 degrees is a relatively good angle to aim for in the beginning.

If the average boat is pointed higher than 45 degrees to the wind, the sails will begin to stop filling and become less efficient. The speed will then drop. While it is impossible to 'see' the wind, its effect is readily seen. As the boat is slowly pointed higher into the

wind, the leading parts of the sails, behind the luffs, will begin to distort and invert and the sail is said to be luffing or stalling. Turning the boat slightly away from the wind will refill the sails and the boat's speed will again pick up. The skill of sailing to

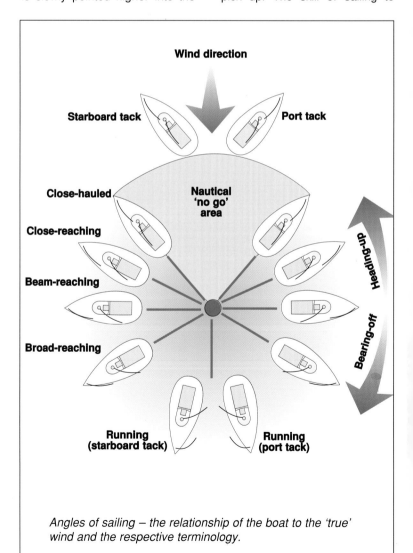

Angles of sailing – the relationship of the boat to the 'true' wind and the respective terminology.

windward is to sail as close to the wind as possible and maintain a high speed. The phrase, 'sailing close to the wind', has come to mean attempting something very tricky that might not come off. It is exactly what sailing to windward appears to be to the beginner.

There is, however, considerable drag from the sails, the hull and the underwater foils when a boat is sailing to windward. These drag forces become lessened as the boat is headed away from the wind and thus the speed of the boat increases. But running before the wind is not necessarily the fastest point of sailing, because the apparent wind speed is reduced as the boat speeds away from the wind. For example, a boat doing 10 knots straight downwind in 25 knots of true wind will have only 15 knots of apparent wind. Going to windward at seven knots in the same conditions, the apparent wind is 30 knots.

In the extreme, however, running can be the fastest as the crews of the boats which race across the wastes of the Southern Ocean in the Whitbread Round the World Race are only to pleased to tell. With strong gales and carrying a great deal of sail, they are able to surf on the waves and achieve high speeds. In the 1993/94 race, on the leg from Auckland to Punta del Este, Lawrie Smith and the crew of *Intrum Justitia* averaged 17.86 knots for 24 hours to establish a world record for monohulled yachts of 428.7 nautical miles in the period. Near the finish of that same race, as the boats approached the finish, Chris Dickson's *Tokio* rode the front of a gale along the south coast of England, and came close to Smith's record. In one six-hour period, *Tokio* covered 126 nautical miles, an average of 21 knots!

There are natural limits to the amount of wind a boat can take. In most cases, when going to windward, too much wind from a gust, for example, can be countered by turning the boat (or luffing) slightly into the wind, or easing the sails. If the boat heels too much, a further alternative to reducing the power of the sails by easing them is to reduce their size. This is achieved by reefing the mainsail – either by rolling it around the boom or by utilizing the reef points in the sail and attaching it at the boom to a point higher up the luff than the tack, and to the outboard end of the boom to a point higher up the leech where the sailmaker will have placed specially reinforced eyelets. In addition, the headsail may be changed for a smaller one. These various processes are known as reefing.

In centreboard dinghies, and a few keelboats, too much wind can result in a capsize unless judicious reefing is applied. For keelboats, which become full of water, this can result in sinking, and is thus to be discouraged: but for dinghies, which have buoyancy chambers in their hulls, it is generally only an embarrassment and there can be very few dinghy sailors to whom it has never happened. Righting a capsized dinghy is a relatively simple matter and is discussed in Chapter Fourteen.

Chris Dickson's Tokio, *a Whitbread 60, blasting up the Solent to finish the 1993/4 Whitbread Round the World Race. Bowman Ken Hara is out at the end of the spinnaker boom ready to trip the sail away. It needed 30 knots from the accompanying powerboat to keep up with* Tokio *that morning.*

CHAPTER FOUR
Things that Can Go Wrong
I Didn't Mean to Do It

Things will go wrong, certainly in the early days of sailing. No one can be expected to remember it all at once, but there are some basic 'musts' which, if obeyed, will keep even the beginner out of trouble. Among them is a recognition that the sea is master and deserves the utmost respect. This is almost as true for a sheltered lake, since it is possible to drown in a small puddle of water; but the broader expanses of the sea are more dangerous still.

Never, ever (and this time we mean NEVER) be foolhardy in a boat. Your own life and the lives of other people on board can be put at risk and when novices are learning the risks are even greater. Not that this should put anyone off, but an appreciation of all potential dangers must be well understood.

Most of the problems in the early stages spring from frustrations induced by a lack of knowledge and experience and can be easily overcome. One of them is an inability to turn the boat in either direction because it is not moving through the water. In this respect, a boat and a car are very similar – one can sit behind the wheel of a stationary car and however much the wheel is turned, the car will not move. The same is true for a boat.

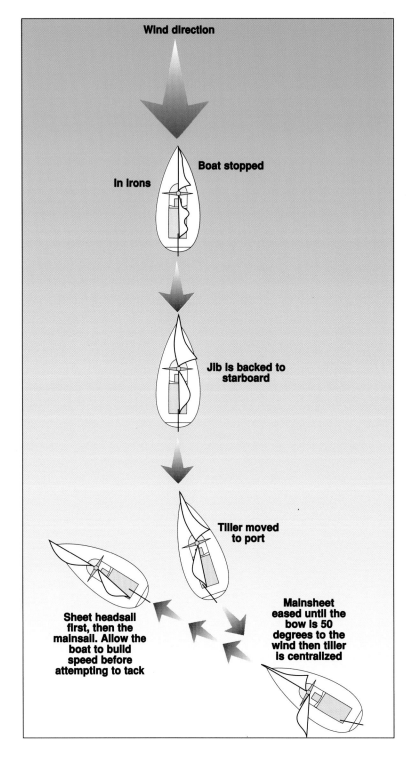

Wind direction

In Irons — Boat stopped

Jib is backed to starboard

Tiller moved to port

Sheet headsail first, then the mainsail. Allow the boat to build speed before attempting to tack

Mainsheet eased until the bow is 50 degrees to the wind then tiller is centralized

Worst of all is the situation when the boat is pointed dead into the wind – the time when a boat is said to be 'in irons'. This is when the sails will begin to flap vigorously, making an alarming amount of noise and inducing panic: there is no need to worry – it sounds worse than it really is and a few careful manoeuvres will soon have the boat under way.

Firstly, because the wind is blowing from ahead, it is likely that the boat may be moving slowly backwards and if one has just pushed off from the shore, that is the very last thing that is wanted. The backwards motion should be utilized to advantage. Instead of steering the boat in the way that one wants to go, by turning the wheel towards the desired direction or pulling the tiller away from it, the opposite action should be taken, both firmly and gently.

A boat going backwards has the water flowing in the normally reverse direction over its rudder. By putting the rudder in what seems to be the wrong way, the boat will, while it is still going backwards, head the way it is required to go. But then the sails begin to fill and the boat starts to go forward – that is when the rudder has to be changed from one side to the other, again, gently but firmly.

Not that this alone will have

the boat heading the right way and moving forward, there are other necessary actions. The mainsheet should be completely eased, and to help the boat to sail backwards, the boom can be pushed forward against the wind. In addition, the jib should be sheeted on the opposite side to the mainsail until the head of the boat has payed off to at least 45 degrees to the wind. Then the jib must be sheeted home on the other side before the mainsheet is pulled home.

The effect of these actions can be better seen well clear of the shore on a day with a light to moderate breeze and should indeed be practised to gain confidence in controlling a sailing boat. Most importantly, the effect of changing the trim of the sails can be clearly demonstrated and the exercise of sailing without touching the tiller or wheel should be attempted very early on.

When sailing on a beam reach, the sails should be trimmed so that there is no weight on the tiller or wheel and once the boat is set up in this manner, there are a few experiments to make to demonstrate how changes of sail trim affect the boat.

Easing the mainsheet will upset the balance, putting relatively more pressure on the boat from the jib and the boat will bear away, slowly pivoting around the fulcrum of the keel or centreboard. Pulling the mainsheet in will restore the boat to her proper course. Oversheeting the mainsail – pulling it in too far – will cause the boat to turn into the wind. The boat can then be made to sail closer than it had been before by checking its turning by increasing the trim on the jib, pulling it in slightly. To bear away, back on to the original beam reaching course, the mainsail and then the jib is eased.

It is not too easy at first, but
this exercise probably teaches
a beginner more about the physical effects of sails than any other.
It also, once mastered, ensures
that the sailor can extricate himself from most of the messes he is
likely to put himself into without
too much trouble.

One must avoid putting the
boat anywhere into the 90-degree
arc where it will not sail – 45
degrees either side of the direction of the true wind – a sort of
nautical 'no go' area. It is impera-
tive to know where the wind is
coming from, particularly the
angle of the boat to the wind.
A quick look towards the masthead, where there should be
either a flag or some other wind
indicator, will show the relationship of the wind to the boat and if
one has entered the 'no go' area,
pull the tiller away from the sails
or turn the wheel towards them.
This will take the head of
the   boat away from the direction
of the wind and allow the sails
to fill properly.

Another problem encoun-
tered early on is allowing the
boat to heel too much, particularly in a puffy breeze. The wind is
rarely constant in either strength
or direction, which every sailor
readily appreciates after a very
short time afloat, and the sailor
has to be constantly vigilant,
looking for signs everywhere as
to how the wind will change. Most
important is a darkening of the
water indicating an increase in
the strength of the wind.

Darkening of the water was
the cause of a decision made
aboard Australia II in the final
race of the America's Cup 1983,
which changed the face of yacht-
ing history. Rounding the fourth
mark, 59 seconds behind Dennis
Conner's Liberty, with the score
3-3 in races, Australia II's skipper, John Bertrand, was told to
hold his starboard tack by tacti-
cian Hugh Treharne because he
had seen a darkening of the
water out that way. Conner had
gybed on what he felt was a
more direct line to the last turning
mark, but when Australia hit the
new breeze, she picked up sufficient extra speed to pass the
American boat and go on to beat
the Americans for the first time in
132 years.

Anticipation of a change of
breeze is the name of the game.
The crew of a boat should move
towards the weather side or sit
out further as the puff hits the
boat, preferably just before. The
boat should be steered, if going
to windward, slightly closer to the
wind by luffing gently a few
degrees and if it is a very strong
gust, the mainsheet should be
eased. All three of these actions
will take the sting out of the
increased wind.

CHAPTER FIVE
Sailing to Windward
The Eye of the Wind

Sailing to windward is, undoubtedly, the most difficult point of sailing in which to achieve perfection, but it has to be mastered to a reasonable degree. For that reason, it is planned to devote a whole chapter to the whys and wherefores of sailing on the edge of the nautical 'no go' area – approximately 45 degrees either side of the direction of the true wind.

Experienced sailors refer to it as 'sailing uphill' and it certainly can be both physically and mentally demanding, but satisfying to achieve to any degree of perfection. No one ever achieves absolute perfection and one's own level of skill is based simply on how close one can come to it. Managing it reasonably well will suffice for all but the racing sailor, and their near-perfection is achieved by constant practice and considerable experience.

Like all hand-and-eye co-ordinated movement, sailing to windward is largely a matter of 'feel', and the degree to which that feel is appreciated by the sailor is a combination of talent and experience. Some will always be better than others, but a huge improvement in everyone's technique can be achieved by extra concentration. This concentration should be aimed at looking at the sails, the waves, and any indications as

to the way the wind is changing, in both strength and direction.

If the boat in question has a centreboard, it should be fully lowered for sailing to windward to reduce leeway, with the one possible exception of heavy airs. When the wind is very strong, the centreboard should be slightly raised to reduce the weather helm by moving the centre of lateral resistance of the boat further aft. Weather helm is the amount that the tiller has to be pulled towards the helmsman sitting on the weather side of the boat, or the wheel has to be turned towards the sails. A small amount of weather helm is desirable to stop the rudder from stalling, but too much acts as a brake on the boat.

Going to windward, the boat has to be worked all the time against the elements, using what advantages one can derive from them. The sailor stays as close to the edge of the nautical 'no go' area as he can, while at the same time maintaining a good speed. His most visual guides are the 'tell-tales', the woollen threads, on the luff of the headsail. These woollen threads indicate the airflow over the headsail. When the airflow is incorrect, either the helmsman is pointing the boat too close to the wind or too far off it.

The woollen threads are set

RIGHT
The crew of the Mumm 36, No Problem, *spring into action two lengths from the windward mark, but as many as can stay on the windward rail to keep the boat as upright as possible.*

back a few inches from the luff and there should be three pairs of them; one approximately on the line which bisects the foot and the leech of the sail, plus one half-way to the tack and the other half-way to the head. The sail-maker will have put these in place when he made the sail. The centre one is most important for the helmsman when sailing to windward; the other two are for the information of the jib trimmer as to where the sheet lead is placed.

Having accepted that the jib trimmer has done his job correctly and that all three pairs are reacting the same, the helmsman will steer so that both tell-tales are streaming aft. If the windward one drops, the boat is too close to the wind, so the helmsman must bear away. Should the leeward

LEFT
Sitting out is important while going to windward; these two bon viveurs could possibly aid the boat's performance by leaning further back, but the rules of the Etchells 22 class prohibit the use of toe straps to help them.

RIGHT
A modern 'strut' kicking strap which gains power from a whip-on-whip tackle. Behind the kicking strap is the fall of the mainsheet which goes to a block on the deck and then aft to a winch.

one, which the helmsman should be able to see through the translucent sail, or a small circular window which the sailmaker has placed for this purpose, start to drop or point forward, the boat is not being sailed close enough to the wind and the helmsman must correct his course.

At the same time, he should be easing the boat through the faces of waves, taking care not to meet them head on, and then taking the advantage of the downhill side of the back of the wave. This may seem very complicated to start with, but it will come with practice. Try to master sailing to the wind, before tackling waves, with firm but gentle movements of the tiller or wheel.

Leeway, that slipping sideways, is inevitable. It is reduced by putting the centreboard fully down, but never fully eliminated. The boat, therefore, never makes the course at which she is pointed. This is more apparent when sailing to windward, because the leeway angle is greater than on other points of sail – also, the faster the boat is going, the less the leeway. The sideways forces on a boat are about four times those of the forces taking her forward when she is sailing to windward, making it the slowest point of sailing.

The sails should be trimmed in reasonably hard – it is possible to pull them in too hard so that the jib, for example, is hard against the spreaders of the standing rigging and the mainsail board flat. An old yacht hand's expression of the Twenties and Thirties was that 'a woman can't dance in tight stays', his way of saying that a boat had to be given some room to breathe the air coming on to her sails. Overtrimming the sails will stop a boat almost as dead as pointing too high into the wind.

The sails will be set with the halyards tight, the mainsail fully hoisted and the luff of it possibly trimmed to a greater tension using a purchase on the Cunningham hole. The clew should be fully extended along the boom by the outhaul. The more wind, the more tension on the luff and foot of the sails.

One new piece of gear comes into this equation – the vang or kicking strap. Used to hold the boom down, it is a major control of the tension of the leech of the mainsail and thus the shape of the sail itself. In general terms, the harder it is blowing, the tighter the vang needs to be, so that when the mainsheet is eased in a gust, it doesn't immediately become baggy, thereby producing more drag, more heeling moment and less drive. It is as well to note that before bearing away on a reach, the vang should be eased slightly.

CHAPTER SIX
Reaching and Running
More Fun, More Fun...

Reaching and running, the downhill part of sailing, are child's play compared to going to windward, but that is not to say they are without their moments of stress, particularly in strong winds. This is the really enjoyable part of sailing even though there is an old adage that 'Gentlemen do not sail to windward', which, in a nutshell pinpoints where some people think the uncomfortable and less pleasant side of sailing lies.

Reaching, with the wind free (often referred to as a 'soldier's breeze') is the simplest form of sailing, as was discussed in Chapter Two – Getting the Feel. It is also the fastest, because the forces acting on the boat become more unified in producing forward motion rather than pushing the boat sideways. No longer is the boat struggling to go forward, it has a positive urge in the direction the sailor wants it to go.

Boats of moderate or heavy displacement are limited in their maximum speed by the wave-making property of the hull. In broad terms, this maximum speed, in knots, is the square root of twice the waterline length in feet. Thus, a J-24, with a waterline length of 22 feet, should be limited to the square root of 44 or 6.63 knots. Anyone who has sailed this excellent little keelboat will

J-24s reaching under spinnakers, the sheet trimmers standing up to get a better view of the sail. Number 4's spinnaker has collapsed because of the 'dirty air' coming off Number 19's sails.

Zamboni *leads the fleet of Mumm 36s down the run at the Southern Ocean Racing Conference (SORC) off Miami.*

know that it can and does go considerably faster than this, because it is able to plane on the surface rather than being fully immersed.

This phenomenon occurs because the boat has developed considerably more power from its rig than is needed to propel it at 'hull speed' and this power is able to make the hull lift above its normal waterline. This is more common in centreboard dinghies where there is very much less downward force of the weight of the boat, without that of a ballast keel. Even so, small keelboats regularly plane, although it will need a much stronger breeze to make them do so than it will a lighter dinghy.

The sails have to be eased progressively for reaching – the further the boat is off the wind, the further out the sails must be eased. Point the boat in the direction desired, allowing a small amount for leeway and set the sails accordingly. Remember too, if it is a centreboard boat, that the centreboard has to be raised to obtain the best balance; again, the further the boat is off the wind, the further up the centreboard should be hoisted. From then on, it should be plain sailing.

Trimming the sails properly will provide the most efficient sailing and is therefore faster. Even when simply pottering, there is no reason to go slowly deliberately, and it can be argued that to do so is unseamanlike. Trimming the sails is similar to that when going to windward, in that one watches the tell-tales on the jib all the time, but now, the trimmer has to set the sails to the course being steered by the helmsman.

The jib is trimmed so that both the tell-tales are streaming aft, but now, to have all three pairs doing the same thing, it will be necessary to move the lead of the jib sheet forward – easing the sheet

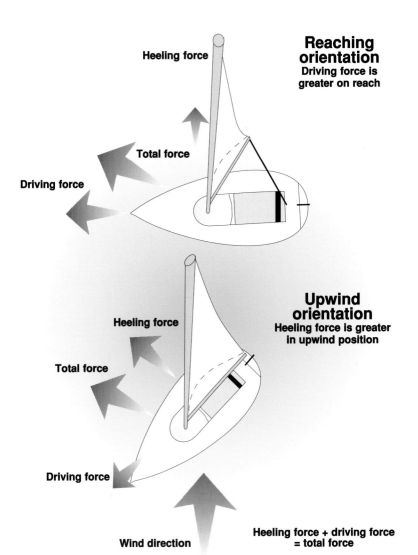

Reaching orientation
Driving force is greater on reach

Heeling force
Total force
Driving force

Upwind orientation
Heeling force is greater in upwind position

Heeling force
Total force
Driving force

Wind direction

Heeling force + driving force = total force

has a greater effect on the leech than the foot and to counteract this and stop the top tell-tales from breaking first, the move of the jib lead is necessary.

When the jib is properly trimmed, the mainsail is trimmed in harmony, eased so that the leading part of the sail is just beginning to luff and then trimmed in slightly. As the breeze is rarely steady, the two sails must be constantly trimmed together, the mainsail following the moves of the jib.

The mainsail is properly trimmed when all the tell-tales on the leech (usually attached at the batten pockets) are streaming aft. The top one is the most important guide and may need ease or trimming of not only the mainsheet but the vang. The wind is not in the same direction all the way up the mainsail for a number of reasons and dependent on the wind strength, the mainsail will need some amount of 'twist', a gradual increase in the angle of attack to the wind the nearer to the top of the sail. Easing the vang increases the twist in the mainsail.

As the reach becomes broader – sailing further off the wind – the possibility occurs for more sail to be set in the form of a spinnaker. The use of this sail is not strictly for the beginner, but it does add greatly to the excitement of sailing and while treating it with some respect (which should not amount to awe), the use of the spinnaker can be mastered relatively easily once its principles are understood.

The spinnaker is not just a bag to catch the wind, trapping it and causing a force in that way, but a sail across which the wind flows in the same way as it does the headsail and the mainsail. Usually, when a spinnaker is set, the headsail is dropped or furled around the forestay to allow a clean flow of air around the major

sail. The light cloth that is used for the manufacture of spinnakers does not necessitate woollen tell-tales; the luff of the sail is very responsive and it is easy to see when the sail is going to stall by the cloth at the luff beginning to curl.

There are two basic types of spinnaker, ones that are the same about the centre vertical axis – symmetrical; and those which are not – asymmetrical. The former is set from a pole of approximately the same length as the distance between the base of the forestay and the fore side of the mast, which is attached to the mast at about the same height, or slightly higher, than the main boom. The symmetrical spinnaker has sheets – and sometimes separate guys (the name given to the sheet on the weather side of a spinnaker) – attached to both clews. The asymmetric spinnaker is most usually set on a longer pole that projects beyond the forestay, often fixed on the centreline, and has two sheets attached to its only clew, the other corner being the tack, which is attached to a line going to the outer end of the pole; one of each of the sheets goes to either side of the boat and the sail is very much like a big jib set free of the forestay.

The spinnaker is hoisted to a defined order after the sheets, guys (in the case of an asymmetric, the tack line instead of the guys) have been attached. Control of the sail depends to a large extent on the halyard and the guy. These, therefore, should be hoisted and trimmed together as the sail goes up and only after they are in order should the sheet (the line to the leeward clew) be trimmed. As a guide, the pole should be set just forward of the line of extension forward of the main boom.

Once the spinnaker is set, the boat will gather considerable

added power and the boat's speed should increase noticeably. Do not try to set one for the first time on a blowy day – the spinnaker is a sail which needs experience to handle. A light to moderate day is best for early experimentation and gaining confidence with experience. As soon as this confidence is gained, every opportunity should be taken to use this sail on a broad reach.

If the wind comes further ahead, or it is necessary to alter course further to windward, the guy is eased (carefully because it is heavily loaded) so that the outboard end of the pole goes forward, and the sheet trimmed home more. If the boat is borne away further or the wind comes aft, the guy is trimmed so that the outboard end of the pole comes aft and the sheet eased.

Normal trim is mainly on the sheet, the trimmer closely watching the weather luff of the sail, easing out the sheet until the cloth just inside the luff tape begins to curl back on itself. Then a slight pull on the sheet will restore the stability of the sail. As a boat is faster with the sheet eased as much as possible (because the vector forces of the sail are greater forwards like this), the world's best spinnaker trimmers always have the luff of the sail just on the curl.

Now the true excitement of sailing can be enjoyed. It is not, however, a perfect world and even greater care must be taken with the spinnaker up, also when taking it down. There is a prescribed order for this, the reverse of hoisting, where the sheet is first eased (to take the weight of the wind out of the sail) and then the halyard, and lastly the guy, are let go. In bigger boats, there are several acknowledged ways of dousing a spinnaker, but these are for more advanced sailors; however, the basic order is the same in every case. Never run a boat dead square to the wind – it is not only slow, but in strong winds it can be dangerous. The spinnaker then does act like a bag trapping wind, but there will still be a flow across the sail and this will change direction frequently and rapidly. In a strong breeze, this can cause the boat to broach out of control, capsize a dinghy and leave a keelboat pinned flat on the water. Never, therefore, run dead downwind but always at an angle to the wind so that the flow across the spinnaker is stable.

Some boats do not set spinnakers and use the jib set to windward to add to their speed downwind. This can be set on a pole, just like a spinnaker, and this spar is called a whisker pole and has a spike at one end, which goes into the clew of the jib, and a hook at the other to go into an eye on the mast. It is not difficult to use and the pole may have to be set well forward if the apparent wind comes round to nearly on the beam – the flag at the masthead gives a perfect indication of the direction of the apparent wind.

LEFT
The crew of Ninety-Seven *about to gybe off Hawaii. The bowman, in the bow pulpit, has the new guy ready to snap into the end of the spinnaker pole, which has just been tripped off the clew of the spinnaker by the mastman. In the cockpit, one crewman will be responsible for lowering the outboard end of the spinnaker boom to the bowman and re-hoisting it as soon as the new guy is 'made' or clipped in.*

DIAGRAM
Reaching – sailing off the wind, the different degrees.

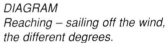
Wind direction

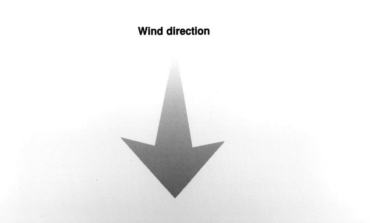
Beam-reaching

Broad-reaching

Close-reaching

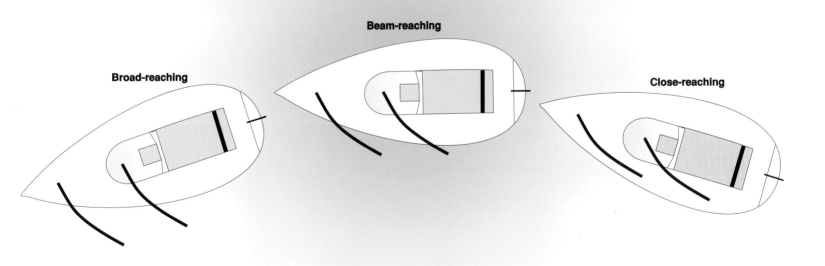

CHAPTER SEVEN

Tacking and Gybing
All Change...

Tacking is essential for getting a boat upwind. We understand that it is impossible to sail dead into the wind – the nautical 'no go' area, 45 degrees either side of the true wind direction, stands in the way of this, and in order to arrive at a place upwind of where we started, it is necessary to tack, often several times. The manoeuvre is relatively easy, but it must be carried out firmly.

It is a safe way to change direction, as the wind comes on the bow of the boat as it changes course and the boat slows down. During a gybe (more of which later), the boat changes direction with the wind going from one side to the other from astern, and this is far more tricky. Tacking, therefore, is always the safe option. In 45 knots of wind, off Muckle Flugga, the northernmost point of the British Isles, during a two-handed race in a 45-foot boat, my partner, Robin Knox-Johnston, and I were faced with a possible gybe, which, if we got it wrong, could have seen us dismasted. Instead, we slowly turned the boat around by tacking – the whole manoeuvre was gentle and we sustained no damage.

Tacking is more normally carried out from being hard on the wind on one tack to a similar course on the other. Coming up to

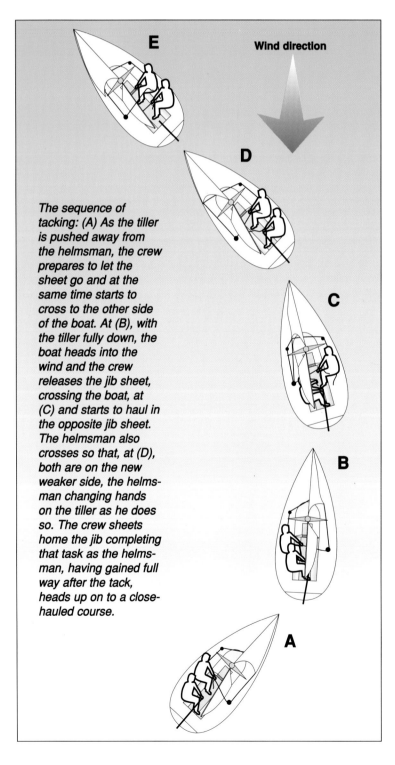

Wind direction

The sequence of tacking: (A) As the tiller is pushed away from the helmsman, the crew prepares to let the sheet go and at the same time starts to cross to the other side of the boat. At (B), with the tiller fully down, the boat heads into the wind and the crew releases the jib sheet, crossing the boat, at (C) and starts to haul in the opposite jib sheet. The helmsman also crosses so that, at (D), both are on the new weaker side, the helmsman changing hands on the tiller as he does so. The crew sheets home the jib completing that task as the helmsman, having gained full way after the tack, heads up on to a close-hauled course.

the close hauled position before a tack, and bearing away from it afterwards are only steering corrections. The tack itself needs precise handling of the boat to make the 90-degree turn and to arrive on the other side of the nautical 'no go' area before gathering full way on the other tack. This is a time when it is vital that orders are heard and understood.

Do not attempt to tack right into the face of a wave. This could easily stop the boat dead in its track and even knock it back on the old tack or, worse still, leave it head to wind, in irons. Look for a flatter than average part of the water, one that will provide the least resistance to the turn, before making any movement with the tiller or wheel. Make sure, too, that there is nothing in the way of where the boat will be going. If there is some distinctive object 90 degrees to windward, make a mental note of it because this is where the boat should be pointing after the tack is complete.

Having alerted the crew with the call of 'Ready about', and received acknowledgement of the call (the crew having checked that both jib sheets are free to run), the next call is 'Lee-oh', as the tiller is pushed towards the sails, or the wheel turned away from them. Neither movement should be jerky, but slowly at first and

LEFT
Andy Beadsworth, Barry Parkin and Adrian Stead, selected as the 1996 British Olympic team, execute a gybe in their Soling, with the Mars *logo on the sail, at Miami Olympic Classes Regatta.*

speeding up as the boat starts to turn.

The boat begins to turn into the wind and the crew should be ready to release the jib sheet fractionally before the bow is pointing at the true wind. This is also the time for the crew to begin moving across to the other side of the boat and he will be followed by the helmsman as the boat begins to come on to the new tack. The crew releases the old jib sheet and turns his attention to the new one as the boat continues to swing through the eye of the wind, by which time he should be on the new weather side of the boat to balance it against the wind. The mainsheet should have been trimmed in slightly as the boat began to turn and eased out more when the boat has passed midway through the tack.

As the sails cross the centreline of the boat, the crew starts to trim the jib into its proper position and the helmsman makes it fully to the weather side, beginning to ease the angle of the rudder as he does so by winding the wheel slowly back or pushing the tiller slowly back towards the sails. He must, however, be certain that he has completed the full 90 degrees, better a little more, so that the boat has full sails on the new tack as they are trimmed home with the boat accelerating

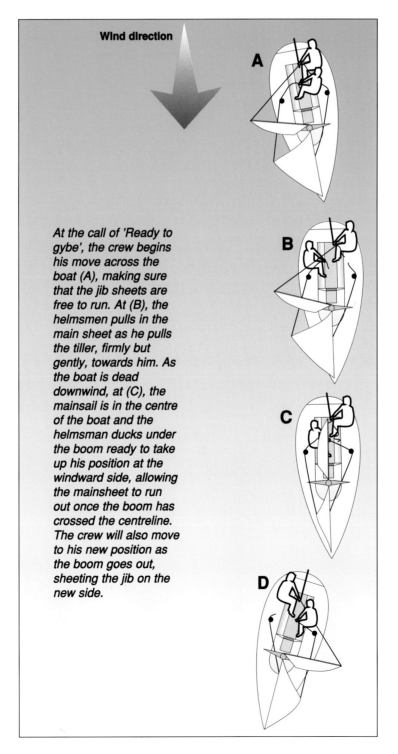

Wind direction

A

B

C

D

At the call of 'Ready to gybe', the crew begins his move across the boat (A), making sure that the jib sheets are free to run. At (B), the helmsmen pulls in the main sheet as he pulls the tiller, firmly but gently, towards him. As the boat is dead downwind, at (C), the mainsail is in the centre of the boat and the helmsman ducks under the boom ready to take up his position at the windward side, allowing the mainsheet to run out once the boom has crossed the centreline. The crew will also move to his new position as the boom goes out, sheeting the jib on the new side.

back to its original speed. The helmsman can then concentrate on bringing it up as close to the wind as he can. It is no use trying to do this before the boat has gathered way or the acceleration will be slow.

Try not to tack again immediately, or the boat will lose a great deal of its speed and be less manoeuvrable. This is particularly important in light winds, when almost all of the boat's speed can be lost during a tack. It is also important that the movement of the people in the boat during a tack should be cat-like; any undue bouncing about can also slow a boat dreadfully.

In light winds, the position of the crew and helmsman may be slightly different, although the helmsman should always sit on the windward side of the boat when beating to windward; the crew, however, may be to leeward to balance the boat. In which case, the crew will still make the first move as it will help to roll the boat round in the tack; the helmsman leaves his move across to the last moment and by doing so will encourage the sails to come up against the wind rather more sharply than they might have done, thereby inducing extra air flow across them and aiding the acceleration of the boat out of the tack. This is known as 'roll tacking' and takes a great deal of practice to perfect.

In the early days of sailing, tacking should be practised frequently, developing a definite rhythm in doing so. It is not difficult but, like every other manoeuvre, it will become more familiar each time it is carried out. Try always to make the manoeuvres smooth but be firm with the steering. The crew should take great care to release the jib at the right time and not to over-trim the new sheet too soon.

Gybing is changing the direction of the boat, bringing the wind on the other side when going downwind. Years ago, beginners were told never to attempt it unless there was no other way out. That only made it even more fearsome than it is, but it is not something to attempt for the first time on a breezy day; only do that when there is sufficient confidence gained by experience from many gybes in lighter winds and progress up the Beaufort Scale slowly, and with trepidation, and always from one very broad reach to another, without a spinnaker, until the manoeuvre is mastered. Trying to gybe from a beam reach to a beam reach, in the early days, can lead to all sorts of problems.

Normally, before a gybe, the helmsman and the crew, of a dinghy at least, will be on opposite sides of the boat. The helmsman will call, 'Ready to gybe' and the crew will acknowledge this before the helmsman makes any move. The mainsheet will be pulled in slowly as the helmsman makes his first move with the tiller, pulling it away from the sails, or turning the wheel towards them. At least half the mainsheet should be recovered before the boat is dead downwind.

It is then that the helmsman and crew start to change sides and whoever is trimming the main sheet should grab hold of all its parts and pull the boom towards

RIGHT
Star 7830 has tacked to port shortly after the start of this race in Biscayne Bay in order to get to the favoured right-hand side of the course.

the centreline of the boat.

This is when it all happens very quickly. As the boom starts to go out on the other side, the helmsman must swiftly move to the new weather side, at the same time centralizing the rudder with the tiller or wheel. It may be necessary, if this last move is made late, to check the boat with some opposite helm movement for a brief second. As weight comes on the mainsheet, it should be allowed to run out, taking some of the force out of the wind.

When it happens properly, it all seems so easy, but there are a host of things which can go wrong. First, the rudder movements should not be hurried or jerky – an abrupt movement can result in the boom swinging over too soon and the boat rounding up sharply and out of control on the new tack (broaching), laying over on its side and possibly capsizing. The boom may not be easy to pull in and it will only come across when the air flow across it has reversed – already the boat is pointing too far away from the wind's direction – and then it will change sides very rapidly and dangerously, almost certainly resulting in a broach. Too little helm movement may also result in the boom swinging uncontrollably or failing to make the gybe altogether.

Do not be put off by one bad gybe, or even several. They have to be practised, perhaps more frequently, because of the danger aspect, than tacks. Practice is the only way to build confidence in boat handling and the more the tricky moves are practised the less problems will occur.

Uffa Fox who, among his other accomplishments, taught Prince Charles to sail, used to say that in moments of stress, such as when gybing, is was 'essential to keep the boat under the mast'. Jeremy Pudney, when he was winning a great proportion of his races in the International 14 class and when they were about to tackle a difficult manoeuvre that might result in a capsize if carried out incorrectly, used to remind his crew, Richard Fleck, with the sharp rejoinder, 'Seamanship Fleck, seamanship'. His crew knew exactly what he meant!

CHAPTER EIGHT
Rigs
The Driving Force...

There is always a degree of compromise associated with sailing and nowhere more so than in choosing the rig of a boat. A boat's rig is selected to fulfil a variety of purposes; it is not there simply to drive the boat as fast as possible, it is designed to achieve the greatest efficiency of handling.

Unless a rig is capable of being properly utilized by the crew aboard, it will always be inefficient and thus counterproductive. The sprit rig of the Thames barge, while appearing somewhat ungainly, evolved from a form that could be best handled by the two-man crew that operated them when they were used commercially. The skipper and his mate could handle these large 50-ton registered craft in ridiculously restricted waters under sail alone.

Today, sailing boats are concentrated in the area of leisure activity and the need for maximum efficiency of handling has resulted in the development of more sophisticated gear. Much larger sail areas can therefore be handled by smaller numbers of crew on a sail plan that gives greater dynamic efficiency. Leading yachtsmen have given serious consideration to making sailing more pleasurable.

Sailing at less than a boat's maximum efficiency is a pointless exercise, yet there are many who are content to do so. Boats with modern rigs should be valued as such leaving those involved in the preservation of traditional craft to their own devices.

Positive advancements have occurred in the design of modern rigs and to the improved hardware now available which makes the handling of sails so much more efficient. No boat should have a sail plan which is beyond the handling capability of its gear or crew. Blocks or winches that are too small, sheets with too few purchases and badly aligned deck gear are simply not acceptable on a boat of any size. Sailing is meant to be a pleasure and anything which detracts from this should be eliminated.

Thus it is that modern rigs have evolved as a measure of aerodynamic efficiency tempered by practical handling ability – an essential compromise. They remain, however, the essential choice of yacht designers and boat owners, and in the case of bigger yachts, the controlling parameter around which the yacht is conceived.

RIGHT
All the sail 'one man and a boy' can handle – the efficiency of the Thames barge's sprit rig is the ease with which sail can be made or stowed.

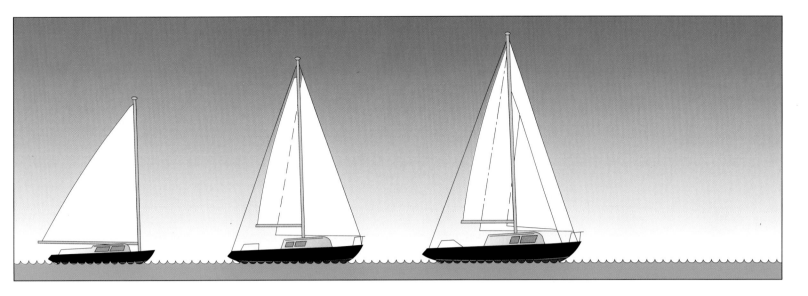

UNA OR CAT RIG

One sail set on a single mast is as simple as a rig can be. Even then it can vary, being set with or without a boom and, in the case of small dinghies such as the Laser, it can be attached to the mast by a sleeve of cloth that envelops the mast rather than being held up by a conventional halyard. Some una rigs, like those developed by Garry Hoyt for the Freedoms, use a wishbone configuration similar to that of a windsurfer instead of a boom, but normally a boom controlled by a mainsheet is the way in which the angle of the sail to the wind is adjusted.

As soon as two sails are set from a single mast, or the boat has more than one mast, each sail will interact with the other and the rig has a more complex wind flow around it.

SLOOP

This is perhaps the most popular rig seen on sailing craft – a mainsail with a jib set ahead of it. The relationship of the two sails can differ and the jib become the more important of the two. The effect of the jib is to accelerate the flow of air over the leeward side of the mainsail in most sloop rigs, but if the jib is the bigger sail, as is sometimes the case with cruiser/racer yachts, the mainsail becomes a flow control for the air going over the sail plan.

In most dinghies, the jib is around half the size of the mainsail and is hoisted only to a point three-quarters of the way to the head of the mast. It is, therefore, crucial to trim this sail in harmony with the mainsail. With a masthead, overlapping sail, the importance of trim becomes dominant on the headsail and the mainsheet trim is dependent far more on how the jib or genoa is sheeted.

CUTTER

The cutter rig has two headsails forward of the mainsail and often sloops will set the extra sail on a temporary stay when sailing a few degrees off the wind. The cutter rig is more common among cruising boats as it allows slightly smaller sails to be set in the foretriangle and at the same time allows for better visibility under the foot of the jib, most generally cut as a high-clewed sail, more efficient for close-reaching than a deck-sweeping genoa. Offshore racing boats, sailing a course just off the wind, will often prefer to use a 'double-head' rig, with a staysail and 'jib top', to having a spinnaker set shy. This is particularly prevalent in blue water events, like the Whitbread Round the World Race, where there is less drain on the physical resources of the crew with a cutter rig than in the constant need to trim a spinnaker. Cruising boats use a cutter rig for similar reasons, but care must be taken to ensure that all three sails are trimmed in concert.

TWO-MASTED RIGS

Using more than one mast is generally a means of reducing the size of individual sails for easier handling but there have been occasions when two-masted rigs have appeared in offshore racing boats as a result of designers exploiting loop holes in the rating rules. The latter have almost certainly been eliminated and the return to single-masted racing boats has been welcomed, particularly by those who crew them, in having fewer sails to trim.

(See over)

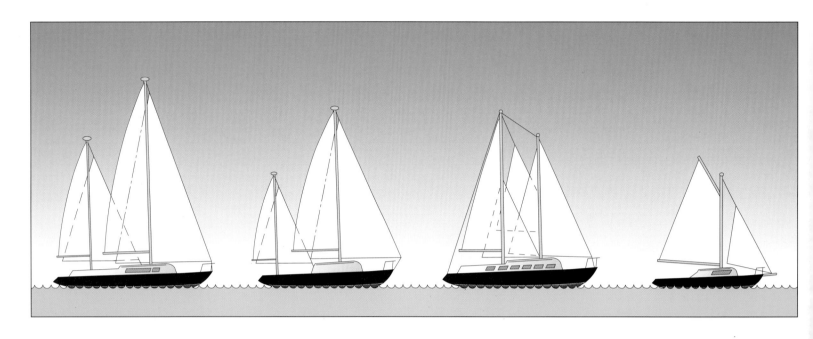

KETCH

A ketch rig has the main mast, the taller of the two forward and the mizzen, or smaller mast, forward of the rudder post. The mizzen, in modern ketch rigs, has approached the same height as the main but is normally around two-thirds of the height of the bigger mast. For many years, mizzen sails were not used up wind, but the development of this rig in offshore racing saw greater use of the mizzen and boats racing in both the 1989/1990 and 1993/94 Whitbread Races were faster upwind by almost a knot when the mizzen was deployed.

Greater use of the mizzen mast is made downwind when staysails may also be set from it and modern development has made these sails extremely powerful. In the case of fractionally rigged ketches, the mizzen staysail area can well exceed that of the spinnaker.

YAWL

In the yawl rig, the main mast is again the taller and the mizzen is stepped aft of the rudder post. Often, this has been a relatively small mast and the mizzen was used to trim the steering characteristics of the yacht. It was a highly popular rig in mid-century in North America, but is relatively uncommon in modern boats. The yawl's mizzen is also used for setting downwind sails, although these are much less beneficial than those of a ketch.

SCHOONER

As soon as the after mast becomes as high or higher than the forward mast, the rig is called schooner. A much loved rig in earlier cruising boats, the schooner offers ample opportunity for the aerodynamicist to investigate the relationships of many sails in the same rig. The aft mast is the main mast and from it is set the mainsail. Often, staysails are set from the forward side of the main mast and are tacked along the centreline as far forward as the heel of the foremast. An inverted quadrilateral staysail may also be set from the main mast head with its upper clew at the foremast head and tacked almost to the deck – this 'Fisherman' staysail is one of the most difficult sails to trim but provides considerable power. On the forward side of the foremast one, two or even three staysails may be set. Experiments have been made to set spinnakers from the head of the main mast but more normally these are set from the foremast of a schooner. Schooners may have more than two masts.

GAFF RIGS

It was an improvement in technology which began to sound the death knell of the gaff rig, though there are those who still favour this 19th-century rig as the 20th century lies in its final death throes, more, it must be said, to perpetuate a tradition than for any other reason. The Bermudan rig is infinitely more efficient. But, according to Winkie Nixon in *Howth, A Centenary of Sailing*, 'the musty atmosphere of 1920's sailing {was} ... a time when all yachts were gaff rigged and people argued endlessly as to whether they should be cutters or yawls ...' Once taller masts could be built, scarfed and glued together from more than one piece of timber, the era of the Marconi or Bermudan rig was born.

The gaff rig has its place in history.

RIGHT
The gaff rig may have its place in history, but there are traditionalists for whom it is remarkably evocative. Tuiga, in 1995 at St. Tropez, is reminiscent of a bygone era.

CHAPTER NINE
Keels
Slip Slidin' Away...

Keels and centreboards have a dual purpose in sailing boats; to stop the boat from going sideways as a result of the forces on the sails and to provide stability, to a greater or lesser extent. The narrower the boat, the greater the ratio of ballast should be, a deep narrow boat having a greater resistance to leeway than a shallow one.

The centreboard dinghy relies almost entirely for its stability on the weight placement of the crew, and, to some extent, so do racing keelboats; but the dinghy's resistance to leeway is almost entirely a factor of the centreboard and rudder. It is extremely important, therefore, that the sections of these foils are carefully chosen and prepared while the surface finish must be ultra-smooth in order that the foils work efficiently to provide lift.

The profile of a dinghy's centreboard is almost certainly controlled by the class rules – it has to be very close to the designed shape, usually within 12mm of tolerance, a shape chosen by the designer because that is the one he believes will be efficient as well as utilitarian. In the way the boat is constructed, the centreboard will have to fit within its case and there will be a rubber or plastic gasket to seal the slot where the

foil emerges from the hull in order to prevent excessive turbulence. Daggerboards, which go up and down vertically in a longitudinally shorter case, are generally parallel-sided for much of their depth and may thus fit very snugly through the slot and not require a gasket at all.

In older boats, centreboards were often made of metal, cast iron or sheet steel, sometimes aluminium. These have a lower

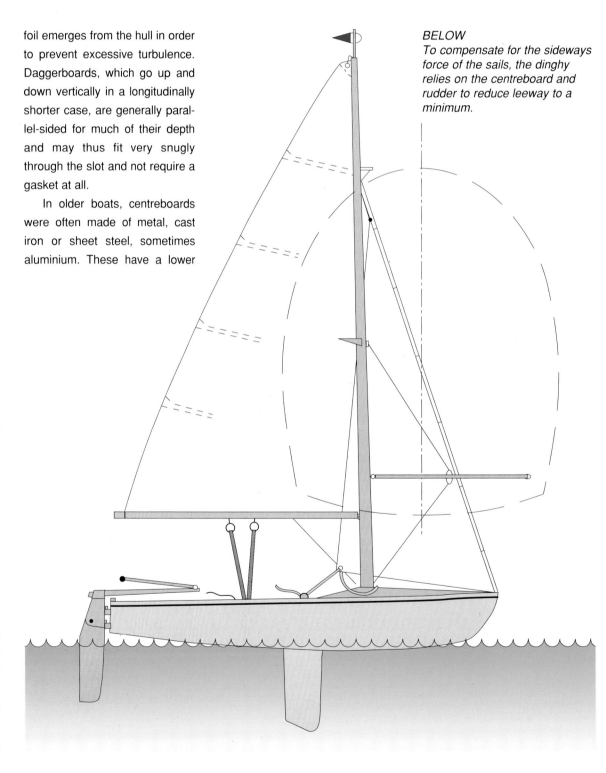

BELOW
To compensate for the sideways force of the sails, the dinghy relies on the centreboard and rudder to reduce leeway to a minimum.

efficiency as they are not an aero-foil section and because of this do not provide the degree of lift of which properly sectioned boards are capable. They still need the same care to prevent unneces-sary drag. Like all centreboards and rudders, they should be paint-ed and filled so that they are smooth and their surfaces bur-nished with fine wet and dry sand-paper (6-800 grit), NEVER wax polished.

Keels come in diverse forms; they may be part of the integral structure of the hull or attached to it. The trend has been towards the latter for the past fifty years, but there appears to be nothing new in this as boats which were racing as much as a century ago had rudders separated from the keel and even turn-of-the-century America's Cup defenders were no more than skimming dishes with huge deep fin keels. In many cases, it has been developing structural technology which has made the naval architects' dreams come true.

RIGHT
The 'secret' winged keel of Australia II, shrouded from prying eyes and camouflaged to deceive. The white painted part would show up to look like a normal keel in aerial photographs.

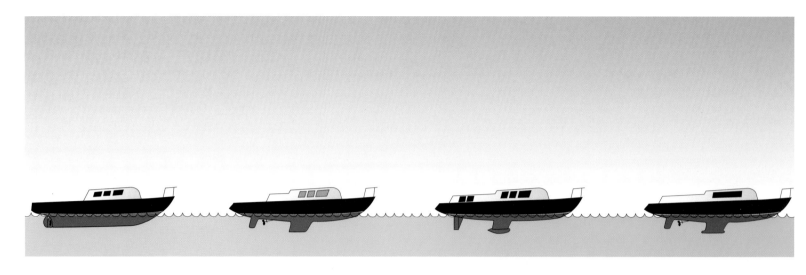

LONG KEELS

The traditional shape developed largely as part of the structure of the boat. At one time, yachts were built, like ships, from the keel upwards; even the lead ballast package was in place as the yacht grew above it. The lead or cast iron part of the keel is bolted to the deadwood and keelson to which the frames are attached, and there is no distinct dividing line between the keel and the hull. The rudder is usually attached to the after end of the keel, even onto the transom of the boat if the keel extends all the way aft.

This type of keel provides considerable longitudinal stability in a yacht, resisting, as it does, the boat deviating from a straight-line course. It is, therefore much preferred by cruising yachtsmen, who find that it makes steering easy or the load on self-steering devices low.

FIN

Far the greatest majority of yachts built today have a separate fin keel. This can be made of cast iron or for more efficiency, lead, and is bolted to the centre-line of the boat through a strengthened structure. Invariably, fin keels are rectangular when viewed from the side and are cast in an aerofoil section. Some racing yachts will have different profiles, but these are minor sophistications, as much in the mind of the designer as in realistic speed improving terms.

The fin keel may have the fore and aft edges parallel – low in sophistication, high in economic value – but more usually the forward edge is raked aft and the aft edge is vertical. The fin is separated from the rudder, which may or may not be hung from a skeg. To a large extent, the shape and thickness of the keel depends on the weight and centre of gravity which the designer is aiming to achieve in order to give the yacht the proper stability.

FIN AND BULB

More efficient, from a stability standpoint, is a fin and bulb keel. The fin can be smaller and thinner, thus having less wetted surface to cause drag and therefore more aerodynamically correct. The bulb, almost invariably of lead, is as low down as possible and provides greater stability for less weight. Quite often, this type of keel is constructed of composite materials, with the fin in steel or fibre reinforced plastics.

Much research has been expended on the shape of bulbs and what began as cylindrical sections are now often flattened vertically to provide a further lift section for the keel.

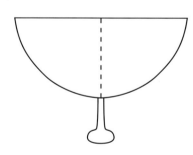

Fin and bulb

WINGED KEELS

A further development of the fin and bulb is the addition of 'wings' to the keel, a practice which became fashionable soon after the Ben Lexcen-designed *Australia II* won the America's Cup in 1983. Lexcen was exploiting the 12-metre class rule, which dates back to 1906, to obtain as much stability as possible for a boat that had maximum sail area within the class rules, without putting its displacement beyond the minimum allowed. The wings of *Australia II* were approximately six feet long and three feet wide on either side of the bulb and made of lead. In addition, the fin part of the keel was narrower where it joined the hull than it was at the bottom where it was joined by the wings. The increased efficiency of water flow claimed for this revolutionary keel, gave it considerably more stability than any keel before it. Consequently, it was always easy in the hazy conditions off Newport, Rhode Island, to pick out *Australia II* at a distance – she was always the most upright of the boats.

Winged keels are not the panacea that many hoped for and subsequent experiments at the highest possible level have produced very mixed results. The flattening of the bulb makes more difference to the hydrodynamic properties of a keel than perhaps the addition of wings.

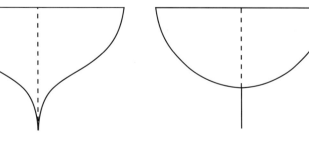

Long keel

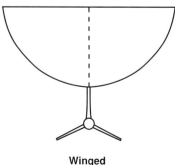

Winged

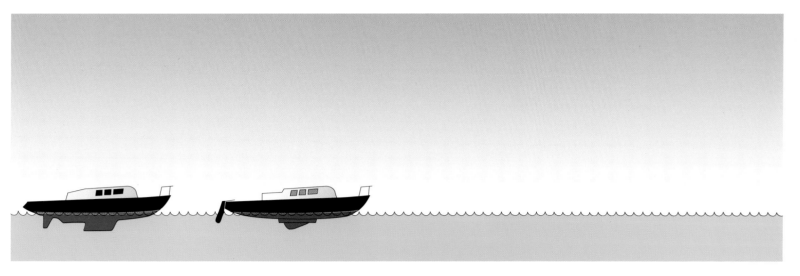

BILGE KEELS

For shoal draft and for boats that have to take the ground, a compromise may be sought in having twin parallel keels attached to the bilges of the boat, separated by approximately a third of the maximum beam of the hull. The keels are placed at a normal distance to the hull surface and positioned so that when the boat adopts her normal angle of heel when going to windward, the leeward one is roughly vertical. They are not as efficient as a single central keel, but they do have their advantages.

LIFTING KEELS

There are many types of lifting keels, many of them centreboards within the keel itself. The centreboard option has always been popular in shallow draft areas, enabling boats to extend their cruising grounds considerably, while increasing their performance to windward by lowering a portion of the keel. This is particularly true of many cruising yachts on the east coast of the United States, where the configuration has achieved a long-held popularity, extending even to racing boats: The Deed of Gift of the America's Cup, as amended in 1887, allows centreboard or sliding keel vessels to compete for the Cup without restriction, and many of the boats from then to 1937 were so equipped.

There are newer lifting keels to be found on light displacement yachts where the displacement is maintained low by having a light bulbed keel of considerable draft. This keel might not be acceptable in many areas where berthing is in relatively shallow water and the keel, normally a parallel-sided fin, is lifted vertically in a trunk, similar to that of a daggerboard on a dinghy, by either a block and tackle system leading to a winch or by hydraulics.

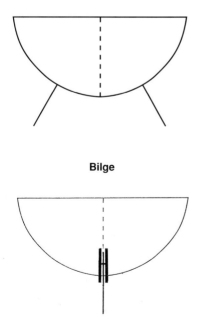

Bilge

Lifting

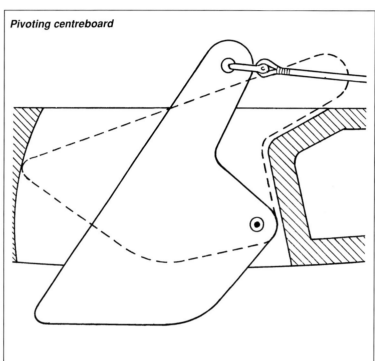

Pivoting centreboard

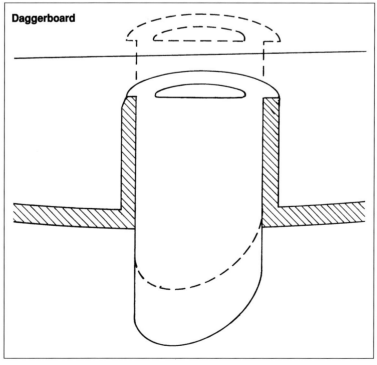

Daggerboard

CHAPTER TEN
Hulls and Gear for the Beginner
Keep it Simple

There are hundreds of different types of hulls and a myriad of boat parts, but a modern boat is the most suitable for the beginner. Most will have similar hardware to one another on their decks and they will be rigged in very much the same way. There is nothing to be gained, for the beginner, in trying to learn on a big boat. Dinghies and small keelboats are ideal and they are uniformly equipped.

Dinghies can be round-bilged, hard- or double-chined. They can be fully decked with a self-draining cockpit, or have only rudimentary decking. Keelboats can be as similar in their cross-sectional hull shape as dinghies, only the form of the keel (see Chapter Nine) makes them very different.

The choice of boat is a matter for the individual, but it is well worth looking at those favoured by sailing schools, where suitability of purpose is the paramount criterion. Even then, the catalogue is long, through every fashion ranging for the beginner. Often, one of the schools' boats can be obtained second-hand for a small sum for someone prepared to do a little maintenance work.

Rod Stephens, the great American designer and yachtsman, was a great believer in the simple approach or KISS (Keep It Simple, Stupid), maintaining that over-complication leads to things going wrong. His advice should be heeded, leaving complex systems to racing sailors who spend as much time working on their boats as they do sailing them. All gear should be practical and functional.

The various pieces of hardware needed on a boat are too numerous for this book to list and investment in one or two catalogues from the major manufacturers, such as Holt-Allen or Harken, is advised. In many cases, they advise on the size and suitability of their fittings together with recommendations for setting up systems that will be all too valuable once a little learning has been absorbed.

RIGHT
The advantage of owning a dinghy is that it can be launched straight from the beach or any other slipway by river, lake or sea.

RIGHT
The traditional long keel gives a boat good directional stability.

BELOW
The bilge keel configuration makes it easier for drying out and the boat is able to stand upright unaided.

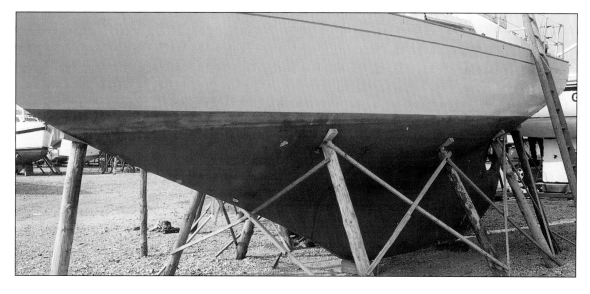

Types of wooden hull construction

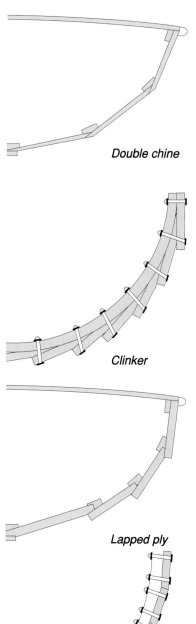

Double chine

Clinker

Single chine

Lapped ply

Carvel

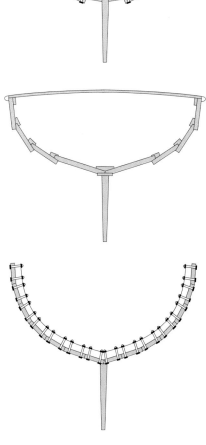

Sailing can be fun for all the family. Catch them young (left) and make sure they wear their buoyancy aids before they go afloat. Race hard, either in a dinghy like the RS 400 (right) or the 28-foot offshore keelboat (above).

CHAPTER ELEVEN
Strong Winds
When the Wind Blows, Our Barge Will Go

Respect for the elements is a primary requirement at sea and the harder it blows, the greater the respect needed. No one is ever going to master the elements, but they can be turned to our advantage, their disadvantages being largely nullified by seamanship. True, with the wind howling in the rigging and the waves building to awesome heights, there are moments when fear begins to creep into the scenario, but those occasions should be few and far between.

Weather forecasting, while not being an exact science, is improving to the point where severe weather is well predicted and those going afloat should always consult the best meteorological information available. That way, they can choose to remain ashore when furious winds are forecasted – no one should ever think of setting out in a full gale. These are the extreme conditions, but there will be times when the wind is strong and sailing has to be undertaken. Everyone who goes afloat should know how to deal with an increasing wind.

In dinghies, where there is rarely provision to reef, the techniques of staying upright and making progress – the two essential requirements in strong winds – rely on flattening sails and maintaining control. To reduce the power of the headsail, the jib sheet fairlead should be moved forward, and, if possible, outboard. This has the effect of twisting off the sail so that the leech exhausts the wind more easily and allows the mainsheet to be eased without choking the slot between the two sails. The outhaul on the mainsail should be taken as far out as possible – this helps to flatten the sail and thereby reduce the sideways force – and the luff tensioned, using the Cunningham hole tackle. The mainsheet traveller should be allowed to go further outboard – again, the harder it blows, the further outboard – and the vang kept tight at all times with a little less tension downwind than when going to windward.

Do not run dead downwind – this will almost certainly result in a broach; possibly the worst is a gybe broach resulting in a capsize to windward. Reach and avoid gybing. This is one time when rounding up (slowly), tacking and bearing away are judicious.

In keelboats, there is a standard order of dealing with a rising wind. The first step will be to make the same adjustments as on a dinghy, but almost as soon as that is necessary, a change of headsail to a smaller one will be due. Headsails are numbered, usually 1-4, the smaller numbers

DIAGRAM
Reefing the mainsail step-by-step.

BELOW
12-metres running at full speed before the strong wind of the Fremantle Doctor *at the 1986 12-Metre World Championship.*

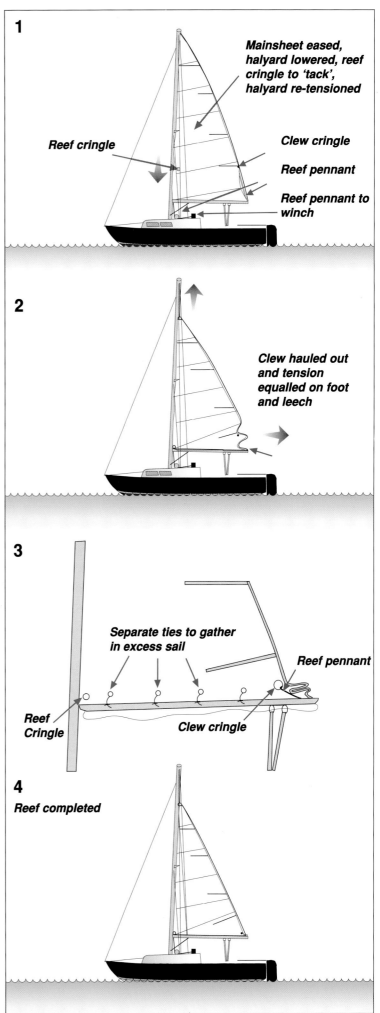

1

Mainsheet eased, halyard lowered, reef cringle to 'tack', halyard re-tensioned

Reef cringle

Clew cringle

Reef pennant

Reef pennant to winch

2

Clew hauled out and tension equalled on foot and leech

3

Separate ties to gather in excess sail

Reef pennant

Reef Cringle

Clew cringle

4
Reef completed

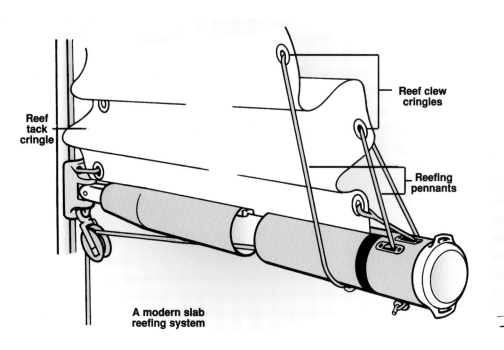

Reef tack cringle

Reef clew cringles

Reefing pennants

A modern slab reefing system

Cunningham hole

Tack

Gooseneck

Slide

Outhaul line

being the bigger sails. Quite often there will be two changes of head-sail before the mainsail is reefed.

With a modern slab reefing system, reducing the size of the mainsail could not be easier. The mainsheet and vang are eased – to take the pressure out of the sail – and then the halyard is freed to allow the luff of the sail to be pulled down so that the reefing cringle can be attached at the inboard end of the boom. The halyard is re-tensioned and the reef line or pennant (which goes from the boom, through a cringle on the leech, back through a sheave at the outboard end of the boom, to the mast and deck) is pulled on hard. The reef is in and the sail can be tidied after the mainsheet and vang have been re-applied. Keelboats often have three or as many as four sets of reef points in their mainsails and the sail may thus be progressively reduced.

Only racing sailors use a spin-naker in strong winds, and then ones made of heavier, stronger cloth than usual. This is when the excitement is at its greatest, but even they can have their moments of upset.

BELOW
One reef tucked in to make this family cruiser comfortable as the Force 4 breeze begins to increase.

The Beaufort Scale

Force	Mean Speed (Knots)	Description	State of Sea	Ashore	Probable Wave Height ft/m	Probable Max. Wave Wave ft/m
0	0-1	Calm	Like a mirror (calm)	Calm; Smoke rises vertically	0/0	0/0
1	1-3	Light air	Ripples only (calm)	Direction of wind shown by smoke	0/0	0/0
2	4-6	Light breeze	Small wavelets, not breaking, smooth	Wind felt on face; leaves rustle	0.7/0.1	1/0.3
3	7-10	Gentle breeze	Large wavelets, crests begin to break;a few white horses, (smooth)	Leaves in constant motion; wind extends light flags	1.2/0.4	3/1
4	11-16	Moderate breeze	Small waves growing longer; fairly frequent white horses, slight	Raises dust; small branches moved		
5	17-21	Fresh breeze	Moderate waves, taking more pronounced form, many white horses, perhaps some spray (moderate)	Small trees in leaf begin to sway; crested wavelets on inland waters	6/2	8/2.5
6	22-27	Strong breeze	Large waves forming; white foam crests more extensive; probably some spray (rough)	Large branches in motion; telephone wires rustle	10/3	13/4
7	28-33	Near gale	Sea heaps up; white foam streaks begin blowing from crests (very rough)	Whole trees in motion; difficult to walk into the wind	18/5.5	25/7.5
8	34-40	Gale	Moderately high waves of greater length; crests break into spindrift with foamy streaks (high)	Twigs break off trees; wind impedes progress	18/5.5	25/7.5
9	41-47	Severe gale	High waves with tumbling crests; dense streaks of foam; spray may effect visibility (very high)	Slight structural damage occurs (e.g. to slates, chimney pots	23/7	33/10
10	48-55	Storm	Very high waves with long overhanging crests, foam making surface of sea white; heavy tumbling sea; visibility affected (very high)	Seldom experienced inland; trees uprooted structural damage occurs	30/9	41/12.5
11	56-63	Violent storm	Exceptionally high waves; sea completely covered with long white patches of foam along direction of wind; visibility affected (phenomenal)	Very rarely experienced; widespread damage caused	36/11	52/16
12	64+	Hurricane	Air filled with foam and spray; sea white with driving spray; visibility very seriously affected (Phenomenal)		46/14	

CHAPTER TWELVE
Clothing
Like a Good Sherry, Light and Dry

Apart from those who wish to believe that the 19th century is still with us, there is no need to appear on any boat looking like a tramp, in old patched clothes. Huge advances have been made in the design and manufacture of clothing specifically made for the sport, the accent being very much on comfort and wearability. No one wants to wear heavy and cumbersome kit and the reluctance to do so often led to being wet and miserable. This, however, was before the advent of foul weather gear as we know it today.

Above all, the sailor should be warm and dry, particularly those who sail in less than perfect climes. It's all very well for the Caribbean sailor to go out in nothing more than shorts, T-shirt and sun cream, but the majority of us need greater protection than these few items can afford. Much, too, depends on the type of boat that is to be sailed when it comes to choosing what to wear. It should be borne in mind that conditions can change rapidly. It will feel considerably cooler going to windward than when running or broad reaching because the apparent wind, and with it the possible chill factor, is greater.

Dinghy sailors have a choice of wet or dry suits. Most usually, they favour dry suits in the colder peri-

ods of the year and wet suits when it is milder. The advantage of a dry suit is that it is just that, and needs only a moderate amount of clothing beneath it, sufficient to keep the body warm. It does, however, tend to encourage the production of sweat and no one should believe they can do a James Bond, peeling off the outer layer to be immediately ready for a martini at the bar. A thermal layer and fibre pile are usual under a dry suit.

Wet suits, most often shortie one-piece outfits, are almost *de rigueur* for the competitive dinghy sailor, and no one knows better how to remain comfortable since he is often on the water for a long time with periods of inactivity between races. These suits do, however, become rapidly anti-social and should be taken to the shower along with their wearer and cleaned just as thoroughly each time after use. It is as well to wear a pair of shorts over the top of a wet suit to protect the neoprene fabric from the battering it would otherwise take from deck fittings.

Side-lacing boots are much favoured by dinghy sailors as they provide protection from the toe-straps as they sit out; these boots are not pulled off by the straps as a step-in boot would be. The choice is varied but there is one essential, they should have non-slip soles.

Keelboat sailors are provided with an even wider choice of clothing and should look towards the three layer system. An inner layer removes (absorbs) any potential sweat which may condense, leaving the skin dry. Should the sweat be allowed to condense, the skin will be left clammy and cold. A second layer should be of polyester pile fabric which helps to maintain a layer of warm air around the body and limbs. An outer layer provides protection from the elements, wind as much as water, and since there are now 'breathable' fabrics, excellent for foul weather gear, nothing else should be considered.

Unless there is a lot of water about on deck, the general preference is for shoes rather than boots. These are lighter and easily dried should they become wet. Uppers should be of good leather and soles non-slip. Boots

will be necessary at times and ones with good soles and that 'breathe' are also available. They must be waterproof and not simply fashionable. One well known manufacturer of foul weather gear decided to add leather boots to his range and was having them made in Italy. When the first trial ones were issued to top sailors for testing, their one complaint was that they leaked badly. They were most stylish and smart enough to be

seen on the marina pontoon but useless for keeping water out. When challenged, the Italian manufacturer, who was proud of his design, merely answered, 'Well, sailing SHOES leak, don't they?'

Gloves, once regarded with a jaundiced eye, are now almost universally worn – choose the kind with leather palms and fabric backs for added protection. For offshore sailing, more water-resistant types with thermal linings are ideal.

Headgear is most important. Almost a third of the body's heat is lost through the head and a thermal hat in winter is as important as foul weather gear. In really bad weather, a sou'wester is recommended – there's nothing so disconcerting as a wet head – and there are specially designed storm caps well worth investigating. In more reasonable weather, a light, long-peaked cap, providing shade from the sun, is recommended. Always attach this to the buttonhole of a shirt with a piece of light line or it will, undoubtedly, blow away.

FAR LEFT
For this Etchells 22 crew, the choice was a mid-weight jacket and high-rise trousers to keep them dry from the spray, and, with the modern fabric, a degree of 'breathability' to keep them dry inside.

ABOVE
Crewman in high-rise trousers, almost always necessary to keep the backside from getting wet, even on the best days.

LEFT
Wild and Wet, but dressed for the ride. The three crewman of this 18-ft skiff are wearing dinghy waterproof trousers (high rise), with specially patched knees and seat to absorb the harsh wear, and waterproof smock tops.

CHAPTER THIRTEEN
Mooring and Anchoring
Home is the Sailor

When sailing a boat away from its anchor, there are certain basic facts that must be observed. The boat will always lie streaming to the tidal current, unless the wind is very, very strong. That will all change the moment a sail is hoisted as the boat will then tend to 'weathercock' to the wind. The routine for raising an anchor, therefore, changes with the relative direction of the wind and current.

If the wind and current are in roughly the same direction, the mainsail can be hoisted before the anchor is weighed (the proper term for lifting it and its chain aboard), but in a crowded anchorage it may be more prudent to hoist only the jib and manoeuvre the boat more slowly until adequate sea room is found when the mainsail may then be set.

If the wind and current are opposed, the jib is the sail to hoist and the anchor should be weighed at the same time. It is far better, if the boat has an engine, to use that, but all sailors should be capable of leaving an anchorage under sail.

Care must be taken when weighing anchor not to bang the flukes of the anchor against the hull. It will almost certainly come to the surface with some mud or sand on it. This should be cleaned by dunking the anchor several times before bringing it aboard. Really sticky mud may need the attention of a scrubbing brush, because, should it get onto sails, it will be impossible to completely remove.

Just occasionally, an anchor is difficult to break out from the bottom, but once the bow of the boat is directly over the anchor, a few sharp pulls should relieve the problem. In rocky areas, a trip line to the crown of the anchor will help should it become snagged in a crevice. This line, which must be attached when the anchor is laid, is a light one terminating in a small buoy.

Coming in to anchor should be carried out from downtide of the desired point of anchorage, remembering that the boat will drop well back from the anchor as a 6 or 7:1 scope of anchor line is necessary – less may be used in very light winds. It should be remembered also that when the tide changes, the boat will swing through 180 degrees to the anchor. If the wind is against the current, and the same applies to picking up a mooring buoy, the mainsail should be dropped early and the anchorage approached under jib alone. If, on the other hand, the wind and current are in roughly the same direction, the anchorage or mooring buoy can be approached with all sails set,

easing the sheets to slow the boat as the mooring or anchorage draws near.

There is a wide choice of anchors and one of the plough types is often favoured. The Bruce anchor, which is approved by Lloyd's Register of Shipping, is a patented version of the plough and is constantly gaining acceptance with much to recommend it. My personal choice is a Fisherman (the shape one immediately thinks of when visualizing an anchor) and I have no hesitation in recommending it.

It is the one anchor that can be trusted in areas of rock and kelp and is approved by the Royal Western Yacht Club, organizers of the two-handed Round Britain Race, for Castlebay, Barra, where such conditions exist. A 50lb-Fisherman held its 45-foot boat in a two-day gale without any problem during the stopover in 1989. The same anchor was used as a brake by the crew of ENZA during their record breaking circumnavigation. It was trailed behind the 90-foot catamaran together with a length of chain in a sailbag to form a drogue as the boat approached the finishing line at Ushant in order to slow her down to prevent a pitchpole capsize in the full force of an Atlantic gale.

Every anchor should have a length of chain attached to it,

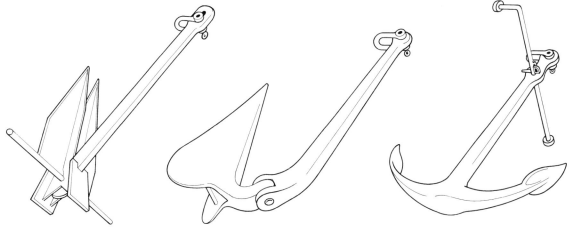

Danforth   *C.Q.R.*   **Fisherman**

LEFT
The types of anchors used by small craft.

BELOW
The tranquil life at anchor, quintessential to a good cruise, but the choice of ground tackle is all-important for peace of mind.

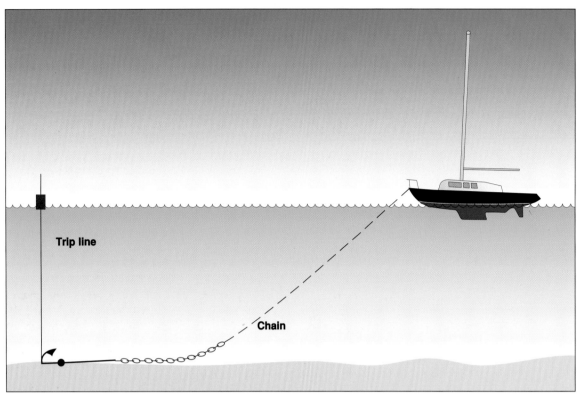

Trip line

Chain

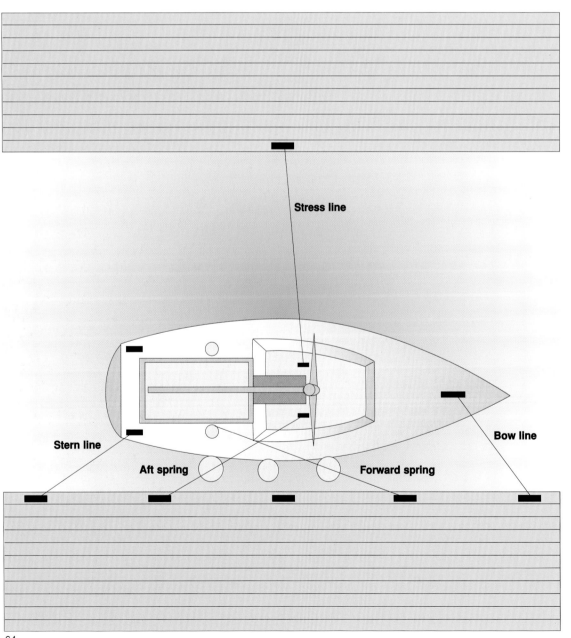

Stress line

Stern line

Aft spring

Forward spring

Bow line

about four to five metres, before the rope line. This helps to keep the pull of the anchor line almost parallel with the sea bed and makes for better holding of the anchor.

Marina operators universally ban sailing within the confines of the marina and thus the question of leaving a dock under sail rarely occurs. It is virtually impossible with the wind blowing directly on to the dock, but otherwise, the sails can be hoisted (and allowed to flap to leeward), the lines singled up, but looped around the cleat on the dock and brought back to the boat, and the head allowed to pay off before casting off. More usually, the boat is taken from the dock under motor power. Remember, always, that when in reverse, the steering works the other way round to normal, and ensure that there are no lines over the side which could become fouled in the propeller.

When docking under power, make sure all the sails are properly stowed beforehand; there is nothing guaranteed to upset the procedure more than sails obscuring the view of the person

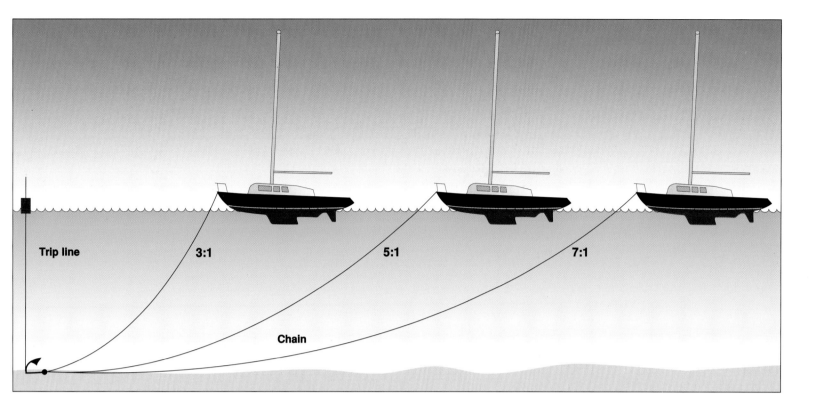

Trip line   3:1   5:1   7:1

Chain

steering the boat. Lines should be at the ready and the fenders in place over the side. The bow line and the aft spring are the first to be attached to the dock; with the engine running slowly ahead, the boat can be held on these tow lines while the other two are attached.

Never leave a boat at a dock or mooring without first checking that all the sea-cocks are closed. There is nothing more embarrassing or needlessly expensive than sinking one's own boat at the dock.

Not only the anchor will need hosing down when it comes back on board...the delight of a lifting keel boat is that one can 'plant' the anchor exactly where one likes, even take it ashore. The lady is carrying a 10-kilo Bruce anchor.

CHAPTER FOURTEEN
Capsizing and Safety
Upright and Honest

Sooner or later, anyone who sails a dinghy will be the victim of a capsize; it is simply a matter of time. Most likely, it will occur very early on and be repeated on several occasions later. This is not the end of the world, even if it seems so at the time, and once a dinghy has been righted and sailed on, the occurrence will be viewed as nothing more than a temporary annoyance and certainly not in any way life threatening.

That is, if one is wearing a personal floatation device – what one in the past generally referred to as a life-jacket – something without which no dinghy sailor should take to the water. The benefit to the beginner is two-fold – to provide a confidence boost and, in moments of extremis, to provide support in the water without sapping vital energy. Modern floatation devices are comfortable to wear, easy to don and afford protection from bruising. There is absolutely no excuse for not wearing one.

Because capsizing a dinghy is so inevitable, righting a boat from this position should be practised in moderate conditions so that the routine becomes second nature. The acknowledged method requires the co-ordination of both helmsman and crew. One or the other, generally the crew, stays in

Righting the boat after a leeward capsize. A. Pulling down on the centreboard and pushing up on the mast to stop the boat inverting. B. Using the jib sheet and the centreboard to right the boat. C. One crew to leeward climbs in as the boat comes upright and the windward crew climbs in over the rail.

the water between the boat and the boom as the boat lays on its side. The other, most usually the helmsman, climbs on to the centreboard or daggerboard and takes the jib sheet on the upper side, pulling it through until the stopper knot comes up against the fairlead (a good reason for always tying a figure-of-eight knot in the end of a jib sheet). Then leaning backwards, taking his weight on the sheet, the helmsman uses his weight to right the boat.

It is prudent, if the capsize happened on a downwind leg, to allow the boat, as it first begins to come upright, to weathercock so that it is pointing into the wind.

That way it will be less difficult to haul upright without the weight of the wind in the sails. As the boat comes upright, the crew can slide into the centre of the cockpit and be scooped up and ready to balance her as the helmsman scrambles in over the gunwhale. These days, most dinghies have self- draining cockpits so that getting sailing again is a painless process.

It is, however, essential to carry certain items on board even a dinghy. A plastic bucket with a strong handle, tied to the boat with a length of line, is necessary for any boat without a self-draining cockpit, to bale the boat after

a capsize, as are a couple of flares, firmly secured to the boat in a waterproof container. In addition, a length of line that can be used to tow the boat should always be taken afloat.

Safety is almost always within the hands of the sailor and rule number one is that he should never leave the boat. There are many recorded instances of small boat sailors drowning when they left their upturned craft to swim to the shore. Far better is to sit it out and wait for rescue, optimizing one's chances of rescue by the judicious use of flares. This is true, too, of bigger boats where remaining with a seemingly sinking boat could still be the best option.

In the 1979 Fastnet Race, in which 303 boats took part, fierce gales with winds reaching force 11 racked the fleet. Twenty-three boats were abandoned or sunk. A total of fifteen lives were lost, seven of them needlessly; they were the crews who took to life-rafts from boats which were sub-sequently recovered. The general consensus is that the only way to enter a life-raft is when one has to step up into it. They are, however, a valuable safety item which should be kept on board any boat that sails offshore and should be serviced annually.

More important on every off-shore keelboat is a harness and life-line for everyone on board

ABOVE
Inflatable buoyancy aids are both comfortable to wear and use.

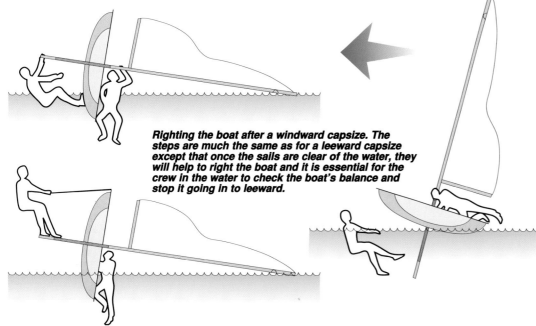

Righting the boat after a windward capsize. The steps are much the same as for a leeward capsize except that once the sails are clear of the water, they will help to right the boat and it is essential for the crew in the water to check the boat's balance and stop it going in to leeward.

LEFT
Using the centreboard and the hiking bars, this single-hander is just at the moment when the boat will spring upright and pivot into the wind.

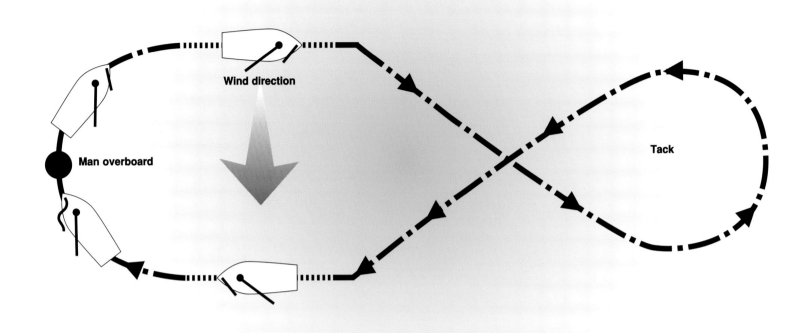

Man overboard with boat going to windward. First put the boat on a reach by bearing away, then dip further off the wind and tack, bearing away again to bring the boat two to three boat lengths to leeward of man in the water and approach slowly to leeward.

Wind direction

Man overboard

Tack

and these should be worn if there is even the slightest doubt regarding safety. Boats do lurch in waves and it is all too easy for the unwary to be thrown overboard. Hitched on with a harness to a strong point on the boat or a specially laid jack-stay, a person going overboard has a 100 percent chance of being recovered; the odds shorten considerably for someone left behind in the wake and for whom the boat has to return. The use of harnesses on ocean racing boats is regular practice and enable a crewman to devote both hands to a task rather than having to use one to support himself.

The drill for recovering a man overboard should be discussed and understood well in advance of an accident actually happening. What the correct method actually is has long been debated by experts but practical experience leads me to believe that the one which has the best chance of suc-

cess is the one we used in the China Sea in the middle of the night, rescuing a man overboard within eight minutes.

On the cry, 'Man overboard' – as chilling a cry as one will ever hear – the helmsman must immediately note his exact compass course. At the same time, another crew member, whose sole task it is to point to the person overboard, must on no account lose sight of the person in the water. The navigator must hit the emergency position button on the GPS and the helmsman will dip a boat's length to leeward before tacking and sailing the boat back towards the casualty on a course reciprocal to the one he had been steering (plus or minus 180 degrees). Picking up one's own wake is most helpful, despite its drift to leeward, as the person in the water will also be drifting in that direction. Approach the person in the water slowly and to windward of them, allowing the

Man overboard

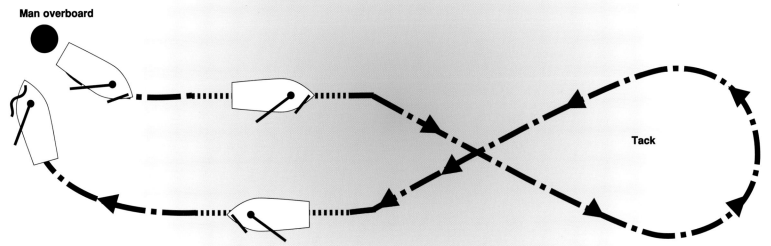

Wind direction

Man overboard with boat on a broad reach. First head up to a beam reach, settle than dip to leeward and tack, bringing the boat on a beam reach to leeward of man in the water, heading up to leeward of him to recover.

Tack

LEFT
Coming out of the cabin to go on watch, the first action is to clip one's safety line to a strong pad eye or jack stay.

RIGHT
The full survival suit in action and no one better than the manufacturing company's managing director, Keith Musto, to test it.

boat to drift towards them and have a line ready to throw to them.

The line should have a large bowline already tied in it so that the person being rescued can easily slip into it and bring it up under his arms. If he is unconscious, it may be necessary for someone to go into the water to help him. The rescuer MUST have a line around his body, preferably attached to a harness, before entering the water. A small jib attached to the side of the boat by the tack and the clew, may be

used to help a heavy person back on board. The sail is attached at the head to a halyard and the person slides into the upper side of the sail and the halyard is hoisted. This will bring the person up to the level of the gunwhale.

Everyone ahould have experience of firing flares, both the parachute variety and the hand-held guidance flare and should know exactly how they work before an emergency occurs. Just how and where to point them is important for their own immediate safety and the general safety of the crew.

No boat should go afloat without a properly equipped first-aid kit. Nor should it set sail without a small tool-kit containing the means of severing the standing rigging in case the boat is dismasted. Should this occur, it will be necessary to clear all the rigging away from the boat before starting the auxilliary engine to avoid it fouling the propeller.

CHAPTER FIFTEEN
Essential knots
Tie Plenty of Them...

There are knots for every purpose – manuals of seamanship are full of them. However, the sailor needs to know only a few of the most essential. It isn't really a good idea to rely on the 'Gary Jobson School of Knots'. Gary, an America's Cup sailor, one-time Naval Academy sailing coach and television commentator, maintained, 'If you don't know the proper knot, tie plenty of the ones you do.'

The ones that are most useful and that you really should know how to tie are listed below:

Figure-of-Eight

Reef

Clove-Hitch

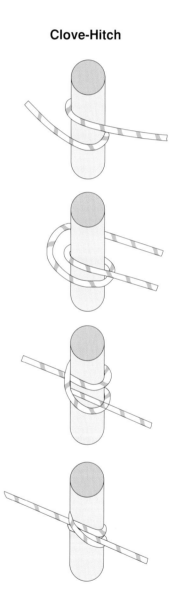

The figure-of-eight is used as a stopper knot in the ends of sheets, halyards and control lines, to stop them running through fairleads, going up the mast or generally becoming unreefed.

The reef knot is for joining two ropes of equal thicknesses. Another version with a slipped end for ease of undoing, is extremely useful for holding something temporarily.

The clove-hitch is used to tie a line to a post or stanchion.

Bowline

Round Turn and Two Half Hitches

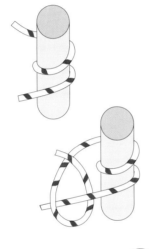

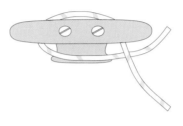

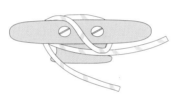

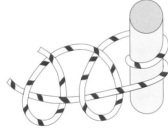

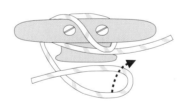

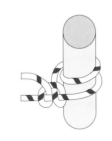

The bowline is the most important of knots. It will not slip and is relatively easy to untie, even after it has been subjected to considerable load. Many, wrongly, see it as a panacea of knots, but there are few times that it cannot be pressed into service.

The round turn and two half hitches is the most secure of knots and is invariably used when mooring a boat to the dock.

Take a full turn round a cleat before beginning to cross the centre each time. Finish with a hitch around the horn of the cleat.

71

CHAPTER SIXTEEN
Buoyage and Navigation
Keep off the Grass

It is important to understand the 'signposts' of the sea. The buoyage systems, and there are two – the American, and the IALA, used for the rest of the world, are relatively easy to comprehend, but it should be seen that the American system views buoys as marks leaving the shore while the IALA views the buoyage approaching the shore. For sailors in the United States, there is the *aide memoire* – 'Red, right, returning' – meaning that the red buoys should be left on the starboard hand when heading into a port, while under the IALA they are left to port. It is almost certainly the huge cost of a changeover which stops the U.S. Coast Guard from falling in line with the rest of the world.

The IALA system of cardinal marks, which have to be left in one or another direction, is simple to understand and was developed to be an international universal buoyage system. It is one of the first pieces of theory that a sailor should master, since by following the buoys he will always keep a sufficient depth of water beneath him.

Charts are maps of the sea and show not only the outlines of the land masses but also the contours of the sea bed. Depths, to a chart datum of approximately the lowest astronomical tide, are marked in metres on the charts; but these will change dependent on the state of the tide.

Tide is the vertical movement of the sea, caused by the gravitational pull of sun and moon, and should not be confused with the current which that vertical movement causes in its ebb and flow. Details of the rise and fall of a particular area may be obtained from a tide table in a nautical almanac and this will also show its relativity to chart datum.

On a particular day, a good estimation of the depth of the water can be gained by adding the base height above the chart datum and an amount dependent on the state of the tide to the depth shown on the chart. The state of the tide can be calculated by the 'Rule of Twelfths'.

Given that the time difference between high and low water is six hours, by using the formula 1-2-3-3-2-1, splitting the total rise and fall into twelfths of that amount and adding $^1/_{12}$ for the first hour after low water, 3 (2+1)/12 for two hours after low water, 6 (1+2+3)/12 for three hours after, etc., the depth at any place on the chart at any time can be swiftly calculated. The tidal stream, the current it causes, also varies in strength commensurate with the 'Rule of Twelfths', the current running three times as strong three

Cardinal Marks

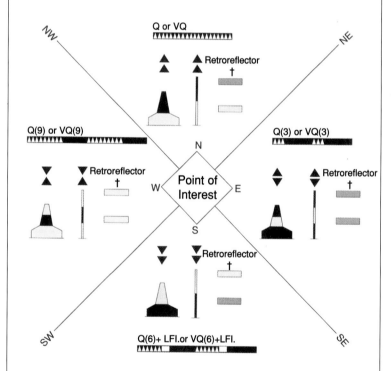

Colour	Black and Yellow
Shape	Pillar or Spar (if a buoy)
Topmark	Two black cones
Retroreflector	Blue and/or Yellow

Notes for all buoy diagrams

LIGHTS, when fitted, are **white** *Very Quick Lights or Quick Lights; a South mark also has a Long Flash immediately following the quick flashes.*

† Retroreflectors illustrated are those of the Comprehensive Code. In the Standard Code these marks are distinguished by one or more white bands, letters, numerals or symbols.

This diagram is schematic and in the case of pillar buoys in particular, their features will vary with the individual design of the buoys in use.

Lateral Marks

Lateral Marks – Used throughout the world except North and South America, Japan and parts of the Far East, where the colours are reversed.

Port Hand
Colour: Red.
Shape: Can, pillar or spar.
Topmark (when fitted) Single red can.
Retroreflector: Red band or square.

Starboard Hand
Colour: Green.
Shape: Conical, pillar or spar.
Topmark (when fitted) Single green cone point upward.
Retroreflector: Green band or triangle.

DIRECTION OF BUOYAGE

LIGHTS, when fitted may have any rhythm other than composite group flashing (2+1) used on modified Lateral marks indicating a preferred channel. Examples are:

Red light

			Green light	
Q.R		*Continuous-quick light*		Q.G
Fl.R		*Single -flashing light*		Fl.G
LFl.R		*Long-flashing light*		LFl.G
Fl(2)R		*Group-flashing light*		Fl(2)G

---

hours after low water as it does one hour after.

Distance on a chart is measured using the degrees of latitude, on the vertical side of the chart. One degree of latitude is sixty nautical miles – and one nautical mile is 6080 feet (a statutory mile is 5280 feet). The metric system is not used to measure distances afloat, only depths. The nautical mile is a defined distance, being that subtended by one minute (one sixtieth of a degree) of latitude on the surface of the earth at sea level. NEVER measure distances using the degrees of longitude, no matter which direction the course is relative to the chart, on the horizontal sides of the chart, as they vary in length depending on the latitude – at 60 degrees north, for example, one nautical mile is almost two minutes of longitude.

Large scale charts will also give details of the type of sea bed, a useful item when anchoring. The depth will also allow the sailor to calculate quickly how much scope of chain and warp he will need to anchor in any particular place.

Chartwork, combined with a log (the regular record of where and what a yacht is doing) is the basis of navigation and pilotage. Prior consultation of charts, the nautical almanac and pilot books, which give details of particular areas, are all necessary for passage making and there is no excuse for not keeping a log on the grounds that the GPS (Global Positioning Satellite) instrument will always indicate where a boat is positioned, as there are times when even electronic instruments fail. Seamanship dictates that the record shall be kept and 'dead

Special Marks

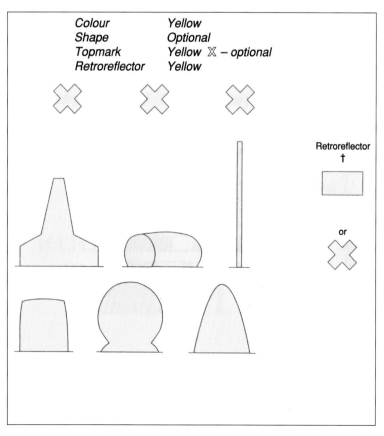

Colour	Yellow
Shape	Optional
Topmark	Yellow X – optional
Retroreflector	Yellow

Retroreflector †

or

Chart Symbols and Abbreviations

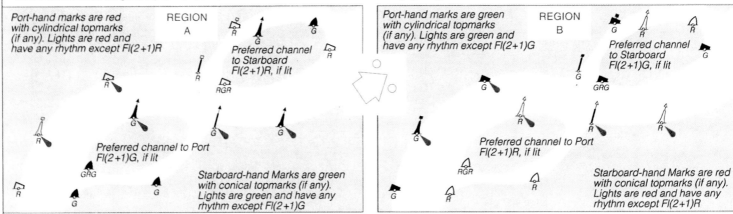

IALA Maritime Buoyage System   *IALA International Association of Lighthouse Authorities*

Where in force, the IALA System applies to all fixed and floating marks except lighthouses, sector lights, leading lights and leading-marks, light vessels and LANBYs.

The standard buoy shapes are cylindrical (can) ⌓, *conical* △, *spherical* ○, *pillar* ⌂, *and spar* ∫, *but variations may occur, for example: light-floats* ⊷.
In the illustrations below, only the standard buoy shapes are used. In the case of fixed beacons (lit or unlit) only the shape of the topmark is of navigational significance.

Lateral marks *are generally for well-defined channels. There are two international Buoyage Regions - A and B - where Lateral marks differ.*

Port-hand marks are red with cylindrical topmarks (if any). Lights are red and have any rhythm except Fl(2+1)R

REGION A

Preferred channel to Starboard Fl(2+1)R, if lit

Preferred channel to Port Fl(2+1)G, if lit

Starboard-hand Marks are green with conical topmarks (if any). Lights are green and have any rhythm except Fl(2+1)G

Port-hand marks are green with cylindrical topmarks (if any). Lights are green and have any rhythm except Fl(2+1)G

REGION B

Preferred channel to Starboard Fl(2+1)G, if lit

Preferred channel to Port Fl(2+1)R, if lit

Starboard-hand Marks are red with conical topmarks (if any). Lights are red and have any rhythm except Fl(2+1)R

A preferred channel buoy may also be a pillar or a spar. All preferred channel marks have three horizontal bands of colour.

Where for exceptional reasons an Authority considers that a green colour for buoys is not satisfactory, black may be used.

 Symbol showing direction of buoyage where not obvious.

 Symbol showing direction of buoyage where not obvious, on multicoloured charts (red and green circles coloured as appropriate).

---

reckoning' observed.

Dead reckoning is the basis of navigation: knowing the speed at which a boat is going and therefore the distance it has covered, is of paramount importance in navigating the ocean when out of sight of land. The navigator will also need to make allowances for the currents, calculating the actual course sailed from vector diagrams of heading and current.

For many years, yacht navigation was regarded as something of a black art, particularly when the mariner was forced to use radio direction-finding beacons as a principal source of information to back his dead reckoning. The use of electronic instruments has made matters a great deal easier, but their accuracy must not always be taken for granted. Reference to the depth can also confirm (or deny) a position on the chart.

In planning a passage, the currents must be taken into con-

sideration when laying-off a course to steer. If, for example, the course to a desired port is almost due south, say 183 degrees, and the tidal flow is approximately west to east on the flood and east to west on the ebb, the actual course steered would depend on the approximate time the passage was expected to take, the speed of the boat and at what part of the tidal cycle the passage was commenced.

Extreme care must be exercised at all times and the person responsible for navigating a yacht should be aware of and conversant with all the aids available to him.

RIGHT
All buoys are identified by their colour and a name or number on them.

Safe Water Marks

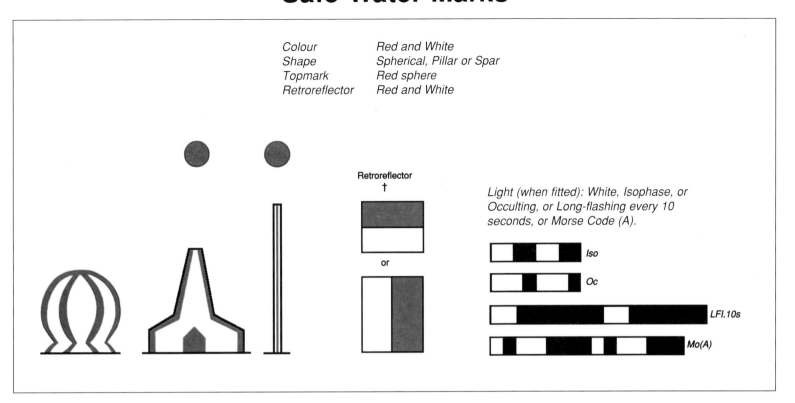

Colour	Red and White
Shape	Spherical, Pillar or Spar
Topmark	Red sphere
Retroreflector	Red and White

Retroreflector
†

or

Light (when fitted): White, Isophase, or Occulting, or Long-flashing every 10 seconds, or Morse Code (A).

Iso

Oc

LFl.10s

Mo(A)

Isolated Danger Marks

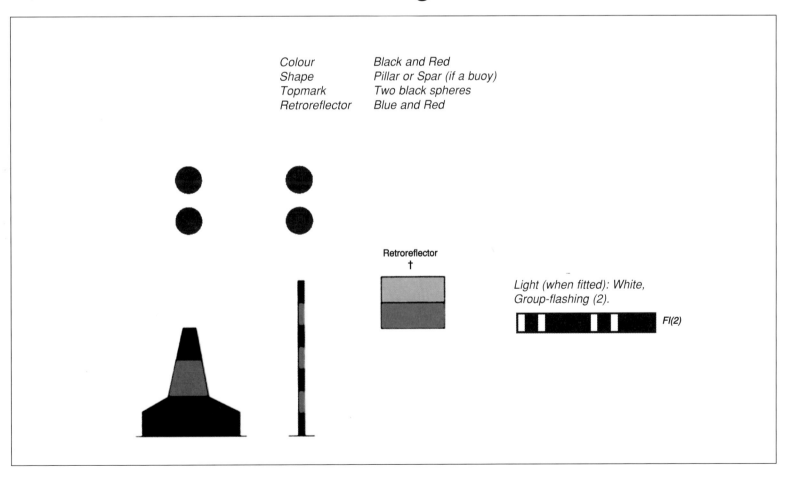

Colour	Black and Red
Shape	Pillar or Spar (if a buoy)
Topmark	Two black spheres
Retroreflector	Blue and Red

Retroreflector
†

Light (when fitted): White, Group-flashing (2).

Fl(2)

NOTE:
Navigational systems have been dealt with only briefly in this book and it is recommended that more detailed learning is obtained before commitment to any long term passage.

System used throughout most of the world

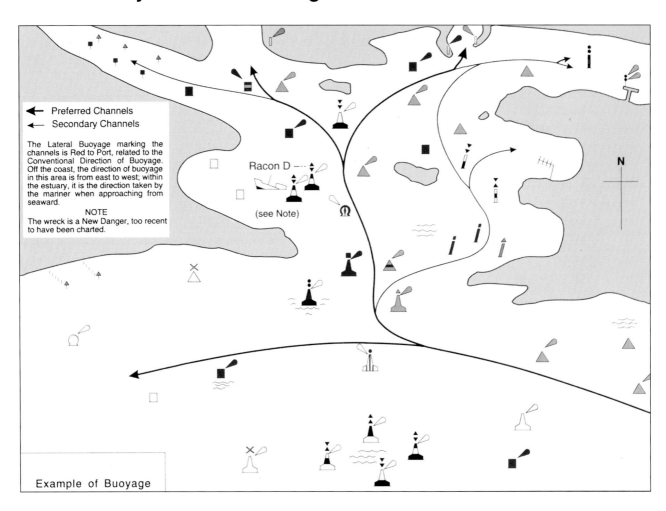

Racon D

(see Note)

Example of Buoyage

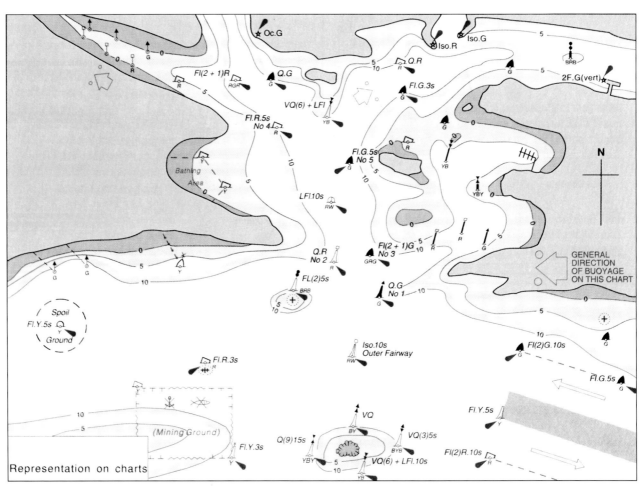

Representation on charts

System used in North and South America and some parts of the Far East

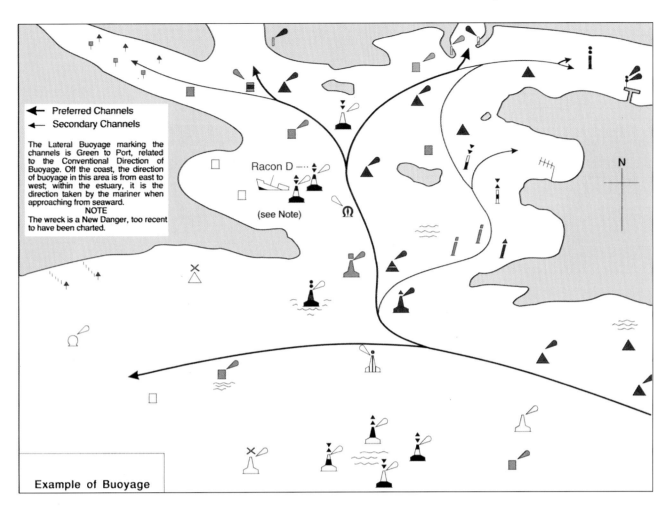

Preferred Channels

Secondary Channels

The Lateral Buoyage marking the channels is Green to Port, related to the Conventional Direction of Buoyage. Off the coast, the direction of buoyage in this area is from east to west; within the estuary, it is the direction taken by the mariner when approaching from seaward.

NOTE
The wreck is a New Danger, too recent to have been charted.

Racon D ---

(see Note)

N

Example of Buoyage

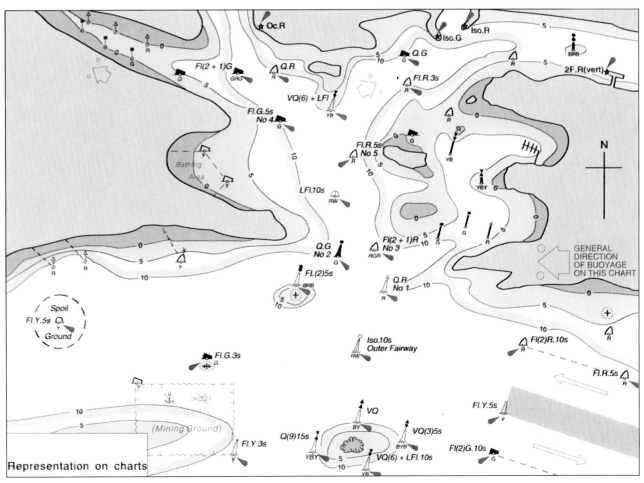

Representation on charts

Glossary

Abaft Towards the stern of a boat.
Abeam Direction at right angles to the line of the keel.
About To go about, to change tack.
Aft At or towards the stern of a boat.
Amidships In the middle of the boat, either longitudinally or laterally.
Astern Backwards, behind the boat.
Athwart From side to side.
Aweigh The action of the anchor as it breaks loose from the ground.

Back The wind is said to back when it shifts anti-clockwise.
Backstay The part of the standing rigging leading aft which takes the strain on the mast.
Bar Ridge of sand or rock fragments formed across the mouth of a river or harbour.
Battens Thin pieces of wood or plastic set into pockets in a sail in order to preserve the shape.
Beacon Navigation aid, either lit or unlit, which is set on the shore or rocks and also acts as a warning of danger.
Beam Extreme width of a vessel.
Bearing Direction of an object at sea expressed in compass notation.
Bear away To put the helm up, keeping farther away from the wind.
Beating Sailing towards the direction of the wind.
Bilges Bottom of the inside of the boat where water collects.
Boltrope A rope sewn around the edge of sails to give them added strength.
Bow Fore end of a boat.
Bowsprit A spar projecting from the bow of a sailing boat from which headsails are set.
Breast line Ropes forward and aft at right angles to the boat to 'breast' into the jetty.
Broach To come up to the wind and get broadside to the wind and sea.
Bulkheads Partitions within a boat's hull or superstructure forming separate compartments.
Buoy A floating beacon with its own distinguishing name, colour, shape or light.
Burgee Small three-cornered pennant flown from a boat usually to indicates the Yacht Club to which the boat's owner belongs.
By the lee When the wind blows over the same side as the mainsail, when running.

Cable A tenth of a nautical mile.
Carry way To continue to move through the water.
Carvel Edge to edge planking used for a boat's hull.
Chain Plates Metal strips fastened to the hull to take the rigging.
Cleat A piece of wood or metal with two arms used for making fast ropes.
Clew The corner of the sail where the leech meets the foot.
Clinker A type of planking where one edge overlaps the other lower plank.

Close hauled Sailing close to the wind.
Counter The overhanging portion of a stern.
Course The direction in which a boat is steered.
Cringle A reinforced eye worked into a sail.
Crown Where the arms of an anchor meet the shank.

Dead Reckoning A position which is obtained by applying courses and distances made through the water from the last known observed position.
Deckhead The underside of a deck.
Downhaul A rope or tackle used to haul down a sail or spar.
Dowse To lower a sail.
Draught The depth of water drawn by a boat.
Drogue A sea anchor.

Ebb The action of the tidal stream as it falls or flows from the land.
Eddy Circular motion of the water unconnected with the general movement of water.
Ensign The flag denoting a boat's nationality and which is always carried on the stern.

Fairlead A means of leading a rope in a more convenient direction and which help it to keep clear of obstructions.
Fathom A nautical measurement of 6ft or 1.83m.
Fender An appliance made of soft rubber or plastic and hung between boat and jetty to prevent chafing.
Fetch To fetch up at or arrive at a desired point or destination.
Fix Obtained by taking accurate bearings or by astronomical observation.
Foot The lower edge of a sail.
Fore and aft In line with the keel, lengthways of the ship.
Forward Towards the bow.
Freeboard The distance, measured in the centre of a boat, from the waterline to the upper deck level.
Freshen The wind freshens as it increases.
Full and Bye Close hauled but with the sails well filled.

Go about To tack.
Gooseneck Universal joint used to secure a boom to a mast.
Goose-winged This shape is achieved when running and the jib is out on the side opposite to the mainsail.
Gunwhale Top rail of a boat.
Guy A rope or wire used to control a spar (usually a spinnaker boom).
Gybe To alter the direction of a boat downwind so that the wind comes from the other side of the boat.
Halyards Lines used to hoist sails.
Head A boat's lavatory.
Heave-to 'Stopping' a sailing boat can be done with the help of the

engine or by laying her on the wind with her helm pushed down to leeward and her sails shortened and so trimmed that as she comes up to the wind she will fall off again on the same tack, thus making no headway. The boat is now said to be 'hove-to'.
Heel When a boat lists from the upright.
Helm The tiller or wheel used for steering the boat.
Holding ground The underwater surface in which an anchor is to be embedded is known as good or bad holding ground.
Hull The structure of a boat below deck level.

In Irons A vessel is said to be in irons when caught head to wind and unable to pay off on either tack.

Jib A triangular sail set forward of the mast.
Jury A makeshift rig to sail the boat to safety after losing a mast or rudder.

Kedge A lightweight anchor.
Kicking strap Tackle to control a boom – also known as a vang.
Knot One nautical mile per hour.

Leech The after side of a fore and aft sail, and the outer sides of a spinnaker.
Lee side The side away from the wind direction.
Lee tide Tidal stream running with the wind.
Leeward (Loo'ard) Towards the sheltered side.
Leeway The sideways drift of a boat from her course to leeward due to wind pressure.
Log An instrument for recording the distance covered by a boat sailing through the water.
Loom The reflection on the clouds when the light is coming from below the horizon.
Lubber's line Black vertical line or mark inside a compass bowl indicating the boat's bow.
Luff To go closer to the wind: also the forward edge of a sail.

Messenger A light line bent onto a larger line.

Neap tides These occur during the first and third quarters of the moon when the pull of the sun is at right angles to that of the moon, causing high water to be lower and low water to be higher than when sun and moon exert their pull in the same direction (spring tides).

Occulting light A navigational light on a lighthouse or lightship in which the period of darkness is shorter than the period of light.

Pintle A vertical pin on which the rudder pivots.

Pitching A boat's movement in a fore and aft direction.
Port The left-hand side of a boat looking forward.
Port tack To sail with the wind on the port side before the beam.

Rake The angle, in relation to the perpendicular, of a boat's mast which can be raked forward or aft.
Reach The course of a sailing boat with the wind aft of close-hauled and forward of running.
Reefing Reducing a sail area by taking it in at the reefing points.
Running rigging Rigging which is not standing, e.g. halyards, lifts and vangs.

Scantlings The dimensions of a boat's building materials.
Sheet Line to control the trim of a sail.
Shroud Standing rigging to support the mast sideways.
Slack water The period when the tide is not rising or falling.
Sound To measure the depth of water by a lead line or electronic device.
Spring A mooring rope. A back spring is led from forward aft or from aft forward.
Spring tides Those tides which rise highest and fall lowest and occur when the moon is full or new.
Stand on Maintain course.
Starboard The right-hand side of a boat facing forward.
Starboard tack With the wind on the starboard side forward of the beam.

Tackle A purchase of ropes and blocks.
Take up To tighten.
Tiller Steering arm attached to the rudder.
Trim To change the set of the sails.
Tumble-home The amount by which the two sides of a boat are brought in towards the centreline after reaching their maximum beam.

Under way This is when a boat has movement through the water.

Veer When the wind shifts in a clockwise direction.

Weather side The side upon which the wind is blowing.
Weather tide Where the tide is making against the wind.
Wind-rode When a boat at anchor is lying to the wind rather than the tide.
Windward The weather side or that from which the wind blows.

Yaw When the boat's head is swung by the action of the waves.
Young Flood The first movements in a flood tide.

Index

Photographic Acknowledgements

Front Cover: Main Picture; Peter Bentley/PPL Limited: Inserts; Jon Nash/PPL Limited, Mark Pepper/PPL Limited, Nick Rain/PPL Limited. **Back Cover:** Barry Pickthall/PPL Limited.

Peter Bentley/PPL Limited; 8, 23, 34 left, 36, 55 bottom, 67 bottom: Bob Fisher; 6-7, 10, 31 top, 32, 33 top, 33 bottom, 35, 41, 43, 53 top, 53 bottom, 56-57, 60, 61 top, 61 bottom, 67 top, 71 right: Bob Fisher/PPL Limited; 24-25, 27: Neil A Foster/PPL Limited; 58, 68: Jono Knight/PPL Limited; 29, 38: Jamie Lawson-Johnston/PPL Limited; 4-5, 30: Roger Lean-Vercoe/PPL Limited; 17: Jon Nash/PPL Limited; 47, 55 top: Mark Pepper/PPL Limited; 2-3, 15, 19: Barry Pickthall/PPL Limited 28, 37, 42, 44, 49, 65, 69, 74: Roy Roberts/PPL Limited 52, 63: Johnathan Smith/PPL Limited; 16: Dave Smyth/PPL Limited; 21, 54: Kim Taylor/PPL Limited; 71 left.